Klein Dytham architecture tokyo calling

**Birkhäuser –
Publishers for Architecture**
Basel • Boston • Berlin
frame magazine
Amsterdam

Workstation (1)

This showroom for Japanese furniture manufacturer Idée occupies the site of an old mom and pop petrol station, which originally consisted of just two pumps and a small two-storey 1960's concrete kiosk. Charmed by the existing structure, KDa opted to retain the kiosk as the office component of the showroom. The new building envelops the kiosk without relying on it structurally.

On the ground- and first floors are the showroom spaces, and on the second floor is a design office. The site is next to a busy road junction with a tangle of electricity poles, and the main façade is composed of a large polycarbonate twin-wall screen, which acts as a filter for the first and second floors of the building and creates a calm and spacious atmosphere inside without shutting out the necessary daylight. From the street outside, the ground-floor showroom is exposed to view, while the upper floors behind the screen offer only a hint of what is inside.

At night the façade becomes a large projection screen on which a play of images, lights, colours, and shadows are visible. When the building is illuminated inside, it becomes a familiar landmark for passing traffic.

In anticipation of a future road-widening scheme, the foundations, structure, staircase and services were designed in such a way that the front of the building can be removed while the rest of the building continues to function.

Location: Shimouma, Setagaya-ku, Tokyo / Client: Idée Co. Ltd / General Contractor: Shinkou Kensetsu / Interior Contractor: Idée Co. Ltd / Start Design: April 1995 / Completion: July 1996 / Floor Area: 193 square metres / Structure: steel frame / Floor: epoxy resin on concrete, expanded metal / Screen: twin-wall polycarbonate (Asahi glass) / Walls: cement panels, coloured film on glass, Made-of-Waste plastic board / Ceiling: profiled steel sheeting / Photography: Katsuhisa Kida, Nacása & Partners

Contents

Workstation	**7**
New Is Now –	
Carolien van Tilburg	17
Kune-Kune Bench	**23**
UK98 Festival Pavilion	**31**
Chu-Coo Chair and Bench	**47**
British Council Information Centre	**63**
A Little Long-Distance Flash of Wit –	
Deyan Sudjic	65
Vrooom!	**71**
Bartle Bogle Hegarty	**87**
Sense of Style –	
Toyo Ito	89
Pika-Pika Pretzel	**103**
Creating a Scene –	
Chiharu Watabe	113
Vegie-To-Go	**119**
Spike Cyberworks	**127**
Wonderwall	**135**
Rin-Rin	**151**
Virgin Atlantic Airways Office	**167**
The Japanese Can-can –	
Klein Dytham architecture	169
Undercover	**175**
Bibliography	137
Colophon	153

Workstation (2)

'When you're a young architect, dying to do wild projects, Tokyo is the perfect city. Just follow the building regulations, and your design can look like anything you want it to'

New Is Now

Carolien van Tilburg visited architects Astrid Klein and Mark Dytham at their Tokyo studio, admired the duo's striking designs, tasted their home brew – compliments of Tokyo Ale – and played with the latest silly gadget to hit Japan.

After studying architecture at the Royal College of Art in London, Astrid Klein (1962) and Mark Dytham (1964) made plans for what they thought would be a three-week tour of Japan in 1989. Their trip was preceded by a flurry of letters and portfolios, all addressed to the various Japanese architects they hoped to meet. No one replied. Refusing to take this lack of response lying down, the persistent youngsters turned to the telephone for a more direct form of contact. Imagine their surprise when enthusiastic voices at the other end of the line assured them they were expected. 'People like Arata Isozaki, Fuhimiko Maki, Toyo Ito, Kenzo Tange, Tadao Ando and both the Suzukis were looking forward to our visit,' says Mark Dytham. 'It was amazing! They hadn't replied to our letters simply because they couldn't write English very well.'

They recall landing in Tokyo and immediately being caught up in the energetic pace and exotic atmosphere of the city. A series of coincidences led to their first job, which appeared within three weeks of their arrival. 'Ito-san [Toyo Ito] wanted to show us a project,' Astrid Klein explains, 'which we assumed was a finished scheme of his own. When we turned up at his office, however, Ito-san wasn't there. We were told that he'd broken his shoulder and was in hospital. While we were there, a guy came in to inquire about the renovation of his wife's hair salon in Ginza. This was the same project that Ito-san had been referring to – it seems that both he and the client thought Mark and I were right for the job.' The next day they visited the site and the following week presented their proposal to the client. 'There we were,' Astrid continues, 'sitting on the tatami in a ryokan, with our first project on the table.' Unable to explain their ideas verbally, the architects had to rely on a series of utterly convincing drawings. It worked. The project was theirs.

17 >> 25

Kune-Kune Bench

KDa was invited to design seating elements for the huge lobby space of a new theatre complex designed by architect Toyo Ito. Contained within the building are a concert hall and two theatres, all of which serve different audiences at different times. Unrestricted by the partitions that commonly clog up public spaces of this kind, KDa designed benches that meander snake-like through the lobby. They can, if needed, serve as partitions. Finished in a kaleidoscopic array of velvet, vinyl, leather and satin materials in matching colours, the swirling snake-shapes leave a lasting impression on visitors.

Location: Nagaoka Lyric Hall, Terashima-cho, Nagaoka city, Niigata prefecture / Client: Nagaoka City / Contractor: Point-Y / Start Design: October 1995 / Completion: October 1996 / Furniture: polyurethane foam on wooden base, steel pipe legs, self-retracting nylon belts / Fabric: bright coloured vinyl, velvet, suede, satin / Photography: Klein Dytham architecture

'There's a lack of context in Tokyo. Whatever you see today may be demolished by next year. Everything is more or less disposable, and change is inevitable. It's a refreshing way to look at architecture'

Having recovered from his injury, Ito asked them to assist him with several other projects. It wasn't long before they had become a permanent part of his staff. 'Ito-san wanted to take on more international projects,' Astrid recalls, 'and we helped him to contact foreign clients by writing letters and so forth. He reciprocated by helping us with our Japanese project.'

The hair salon took about six months to complete, but it was only the first of several projects that came their way during a two-year stint with Ito. 'Working at Ito's office was great,' says Astrid fondly. 'As newcomers to Japan, we came to regard him and his staff as our family. We were very lucky.'

When their three-week tour had stretched into two years, the duo set up their own office but continued to work for Ito on a part-time basis. 'In Japan you can never really leave a place,' Mark says. 'Here, a relationship is forever.'

At one point a developer commissioned them to convert a number of old mansions into new flats, in the manner of the London Docklands. But soon after Japan's economic bubble burst, the banks withdrew all funds and the project stagnated. To make ends meet, KDa (Klein Dytham architecture) did all sorts of jobs, particularly interiors. Born of necessity, this broad-based strategy continues to characterise work produced by a firm that currently boasts a staff of eight.

In 1993 KDa walked off with the Kajima Space Design Award for best young practice in Japan. Three years later, their Idée Workstation won both the Asahi Glass Design Award and the National Panasonic Design Award. In 1998 KDa's interior for a new information centre at the Tokyo British Council received a national award for best library. And the popularity of their website – www.klein-dytham.com – which generates over 10,000 page hits a week, is a prize in itself. A fun feature is a collage of the Tokyo landscape composed of ads, billboards and a potpourri of products.

Astrid Klein, born and raised in Italy by her German parents, graduated from a beaux-arts college in France and went on to study interior design. She has a nose for trends, colours and

UK98 Festival Pavilion (1)

Designed for UK98, a year-long festival of British culture in Japan, this pavilion uses typically British technology. The highly practical and flexible structure avails of such cutting-edge technologies as those developed by yacht-mast specialist Proctor Masts and leading hot-air balloon manufacturer Cameron Balloons.

The demountable pavilion, which was transported around Japan during this year-long festival, can be erected in several different configurations depending on the space available. KDa developed a system of interlocking circles, similar to traditional Japanese trays, which allowed the elements to be arranged in a straight line, radial pattern, curve, or as individual units.

Each circle comes packed in four crates, which form benches when unpacked and which can be filled with water bladders to secure the pavilion in position. Not knowing in advance where the event space was to be erected, KDa came up with an ingenious solution that uses water to anchor the pavilion to any surface. All joints in the aluminium structure use the same tongue-and-groove connection. Each canopy is inflated using a small, permanently powered 150-watt fan. The balloons are illuminated from within by a sodium halide lamp. Once inflated, the balloon is lifted into position on top of the ring structure and secured by an elastic cord, which runs through a series of hooks and eyes. This simple system allows four to six people to erect the whole pavilion in around five hours.

Erected at 35 venues around Japan, the pavilion was ideal for all possible weather conditions, from heavy winds and showers to snow.

Location: 35 locations around Japan / Client: The British Embassy / Balloon Manufacturer: Cameron Balloons / Structural Engineer: Arup Japan / Structural Frame: Devomet / Start Design: April 1997 / Completion: January 1998 / Balloon: hyper last gas fabric, inflated by centrifugal fan / Frame: aluminium pipe / Base/Storage Crate: plywood on steel pipe frame, water bladders / Photography: Katsuhisa Kida, Klein Dytham architecture

A series of coincidences led to their first job,
which appeared within three weeks of their arrival

materials. Mark Dytham, a witty Briton, is the engineering half of the pair, a guy with a fascination for new gadgets and technologies. 'I'm an early adopter,' he says. 'I don't mind if products have growing pains. I like to tackle the flaws and find a solution. The structure of a project and the logic behind it are my main contributions to KDa. I analyse the concept from every possible angle. Astrid is into colour and the kind of quirky stuff that I wouldn't dare put into a project. If I don't like something and can't come up with a better idea, however, I trust Astrid's judgement. We don't compromise.'

Apparently, the balance of responsibility at KDa is based on Mark's supervision of the architectural process and day-to-day affairs and Astrid's role in creating interiors. 'But I do consult Mark on all major decisions,' Astrid assures me.

When KDa discovered a huge automotive repair shop close to the Azabu-Juban intersection in central Tokyo, they jumped at the chance to use it as a workplace. They share the converted premises with five other creative companies: Spinoff (interior design), Namaiki (graphic design), Tokyo Brewing Company, Nakameguro Yakkyoku (DJ and computer graphics) and DoReMi (sound design). This six-faceted collective calls itself Deluxe. Although not a luxurious working environment, the building does offer its occupants a large area for exhibitions and other events. The tenants jokingly claim that beer is the glue that holds them all together.

Mark got involved with the brewery after deciding that regular Japanese beer tastes like an isotonic drink for athletes. 'Being English, I wanted to enjoy a proper pint,' he laughs. 'It all started with a "philosophical" idea.'

'For the time being, it's just a bit of fun – you might call it an entertaining enterprise,' Astrid adds. KDa is always up for a new opportunity. In Tokyo art circles, however, Deluxe is known less for its beer than for its unconventional exhibitions and events. The premier event featured a Swedish artist and his entourage of 2,000 crickets: 1,000 of one species and 1,000 of another. He put the insects together in an acrylic box and called it 'the monsters of rock'. Their battle was purely an

UK98 Festival Pavilion (2)

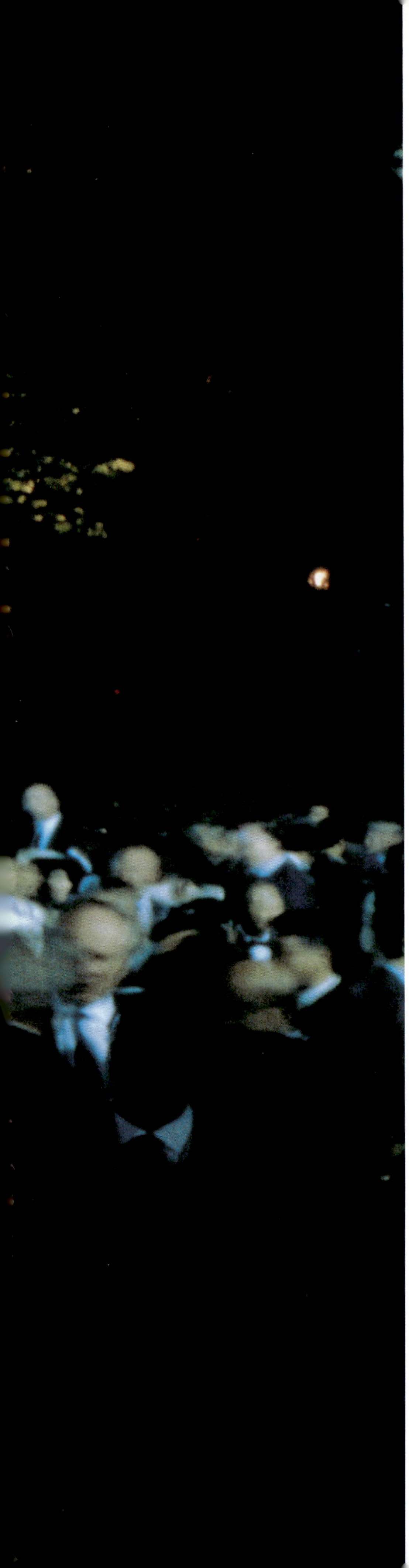

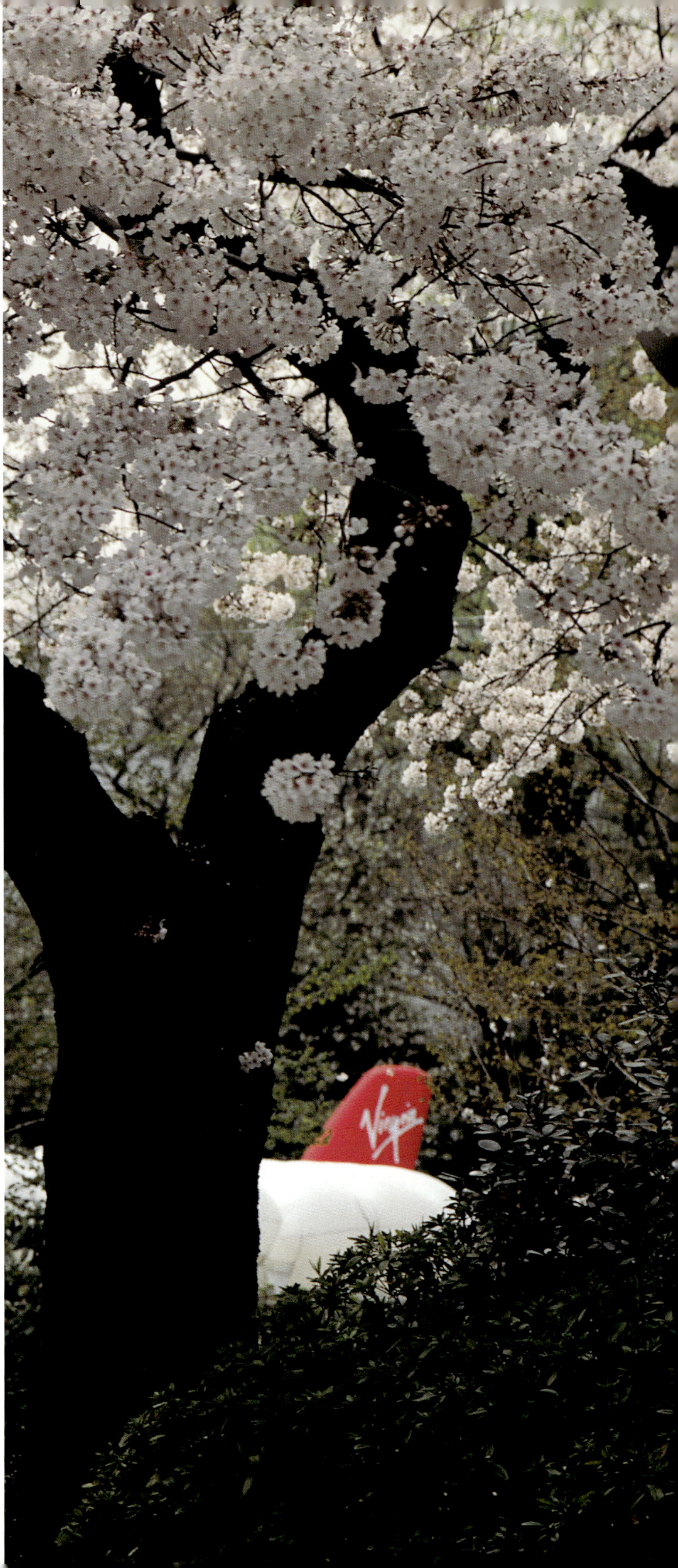
Virgin

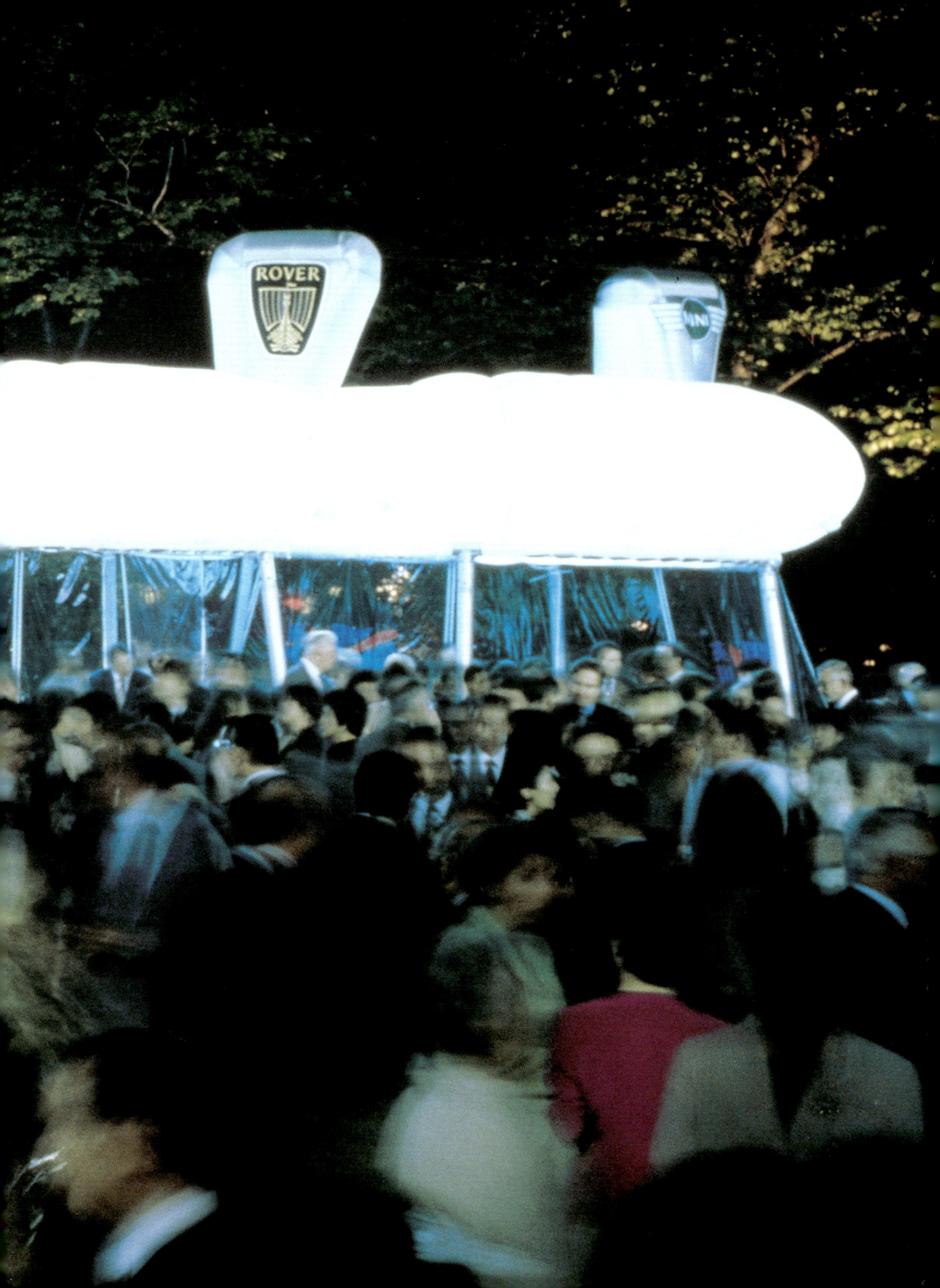
ROVER

'The structure of a project and the logic behind it are my main contributions to Kda,' Mark says. 'I analyse the concept from every possible angle. Astrid is into colour and the kind of quirky stuff that I wouldn't dare put into a project' acoustic competition – a cacophony of sounds that the artist mixed to create a concert. Deluxe has since hosted a string of equally outlandish events.

Sometimes they rent out the space to earn money. 'At other times,' Mark says, 'we don't charge anything. When it's a friend or someone who does good work but can't afford an exhibition space, there's no price tag. We have no fixed policy, and that's what Deluxe is all about.'

Clients may find the location and its facilities slightly unnerving. The open space serves as a meeting room for clients of all six companies, which makes for some pretty strange encounters. 'Once we had an installation on display, with a naked lady in a feather bath hanging from the ceiling,' Mark recollects. 'A client came in from the countryside to meet us. It was only the second time he'd visited Tokyo, and there he was – in the middle of a warehouse with a nude woman tossing feathers from the rafters. The poor guy had a big problem concentrating on the details.' The creative setting provided by Deluxe turns a normal business meeting into a happening. 'Interaction among the six companies is excellent,' Mark continues. 'One firm introduces its clients to the others. Even though we work independently, that kind of networking elevates us as a group. Deluxe has an identity of its own.'

Plans for demolition of the warehouse mean that Deluxe is facing an exciting episode in its evolution: a relocation operation in 2002. The collective has already chosen a new name, SuperDeluxe, but the actual site of their new offices remains unknown. Astrid and Mark like to create projects that make people smile. They want to stir up the kind of fun that promotes a positive image of their client. A prime example is the inflated silver walls they created for a construction site on Omotesando – a dynamic, out-of-the-box design that's easy to understand. 'We try to make things that everyone can enjoy,' Astrid explains. 'We don't want to be elitist, and our approach is far from academic. Architecture is all about the visual; you never find a note inside that describes the concept. Just look at it. See it.'

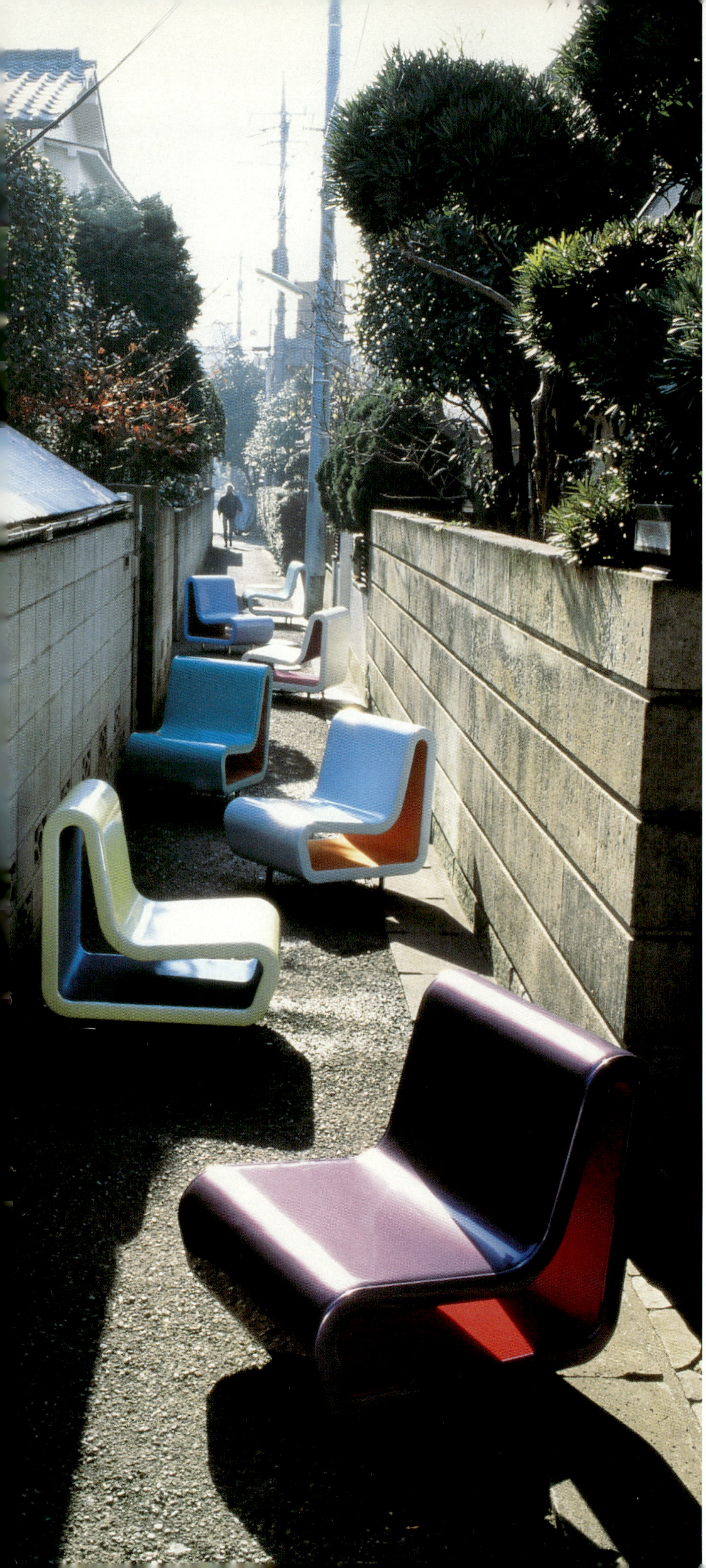

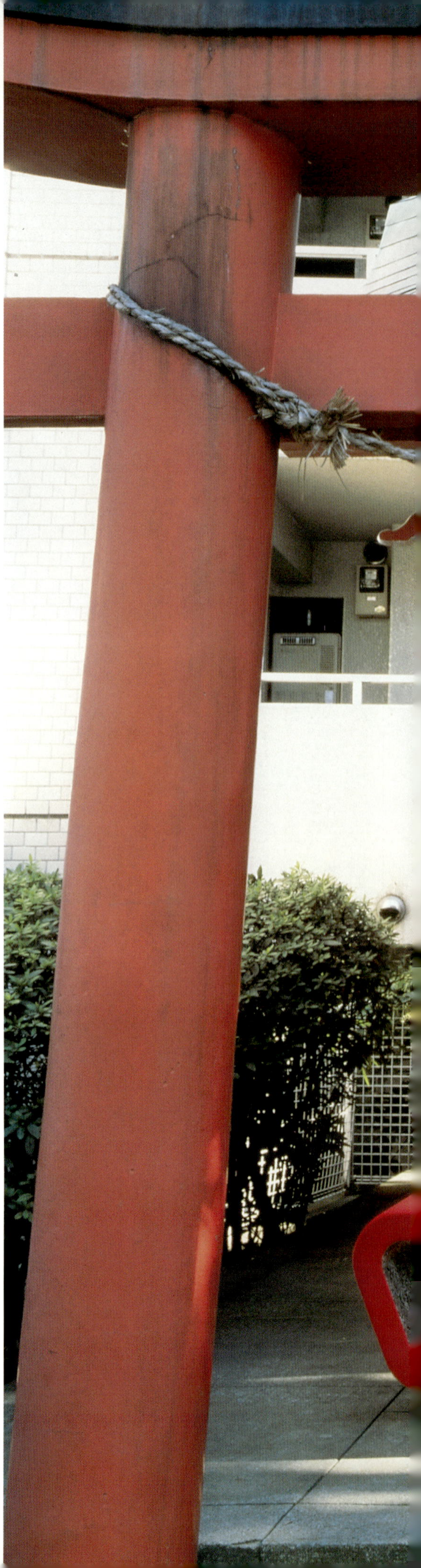

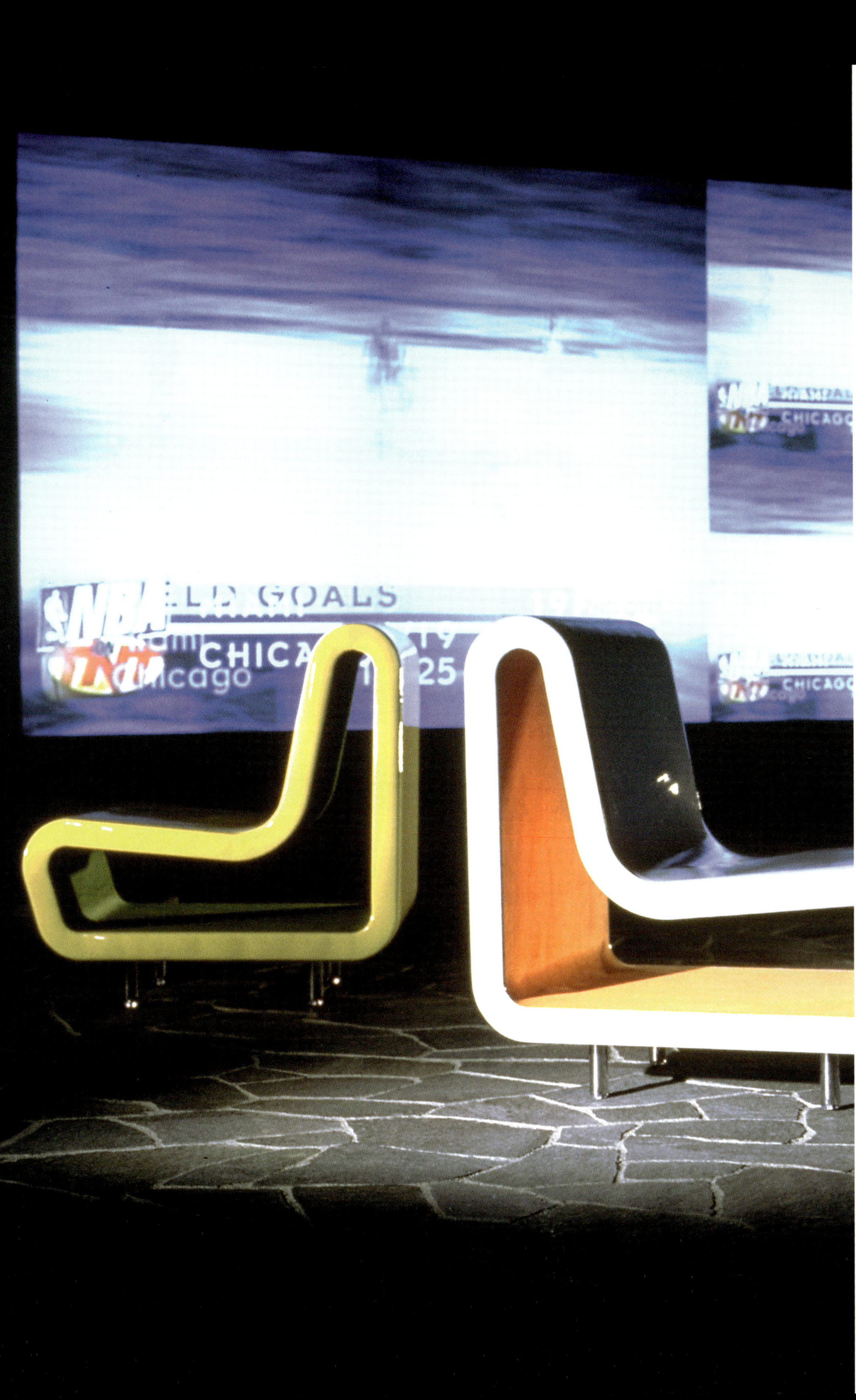
NBA
ELD GOALS
CHICA
Chicago
CHICAGO
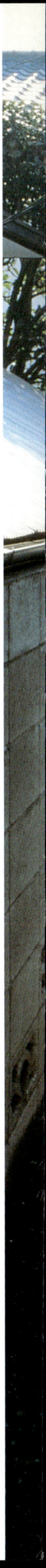

Chu-Coo Chair and Bench (1)

Durability and a touch of glamour are both captured in the Chu-Coo chair. Asked by the public broadcaster NHK to design benches and chairs for their Nagano lobby, KDa chose maintenance-free vinyl covers for these retro-styled chairs. As a luxury alternative, the chairs inside are covered with either velvet or fake snakeskin.
The open structure not only provides handy storage space for magazines, but also makes for a playful object on which to while away the time.

Location: NHK Nagano, Inaba, Nagano city, Nagano prefecture / Client: NHK, Bartle Bogle Hegarty, Laforet, others / Architect: Klein Dytham architecture / Manufacturer: Do-ing / Start Design: September 1997 / Completion: February 1998 / Furniture: polyurethane foam on wooden base, steel pipe legs / Fabric: shiny vinyl, velvet, snakeskin / Photography: Mitsumasa Fujitsuka, Kozo Takayama

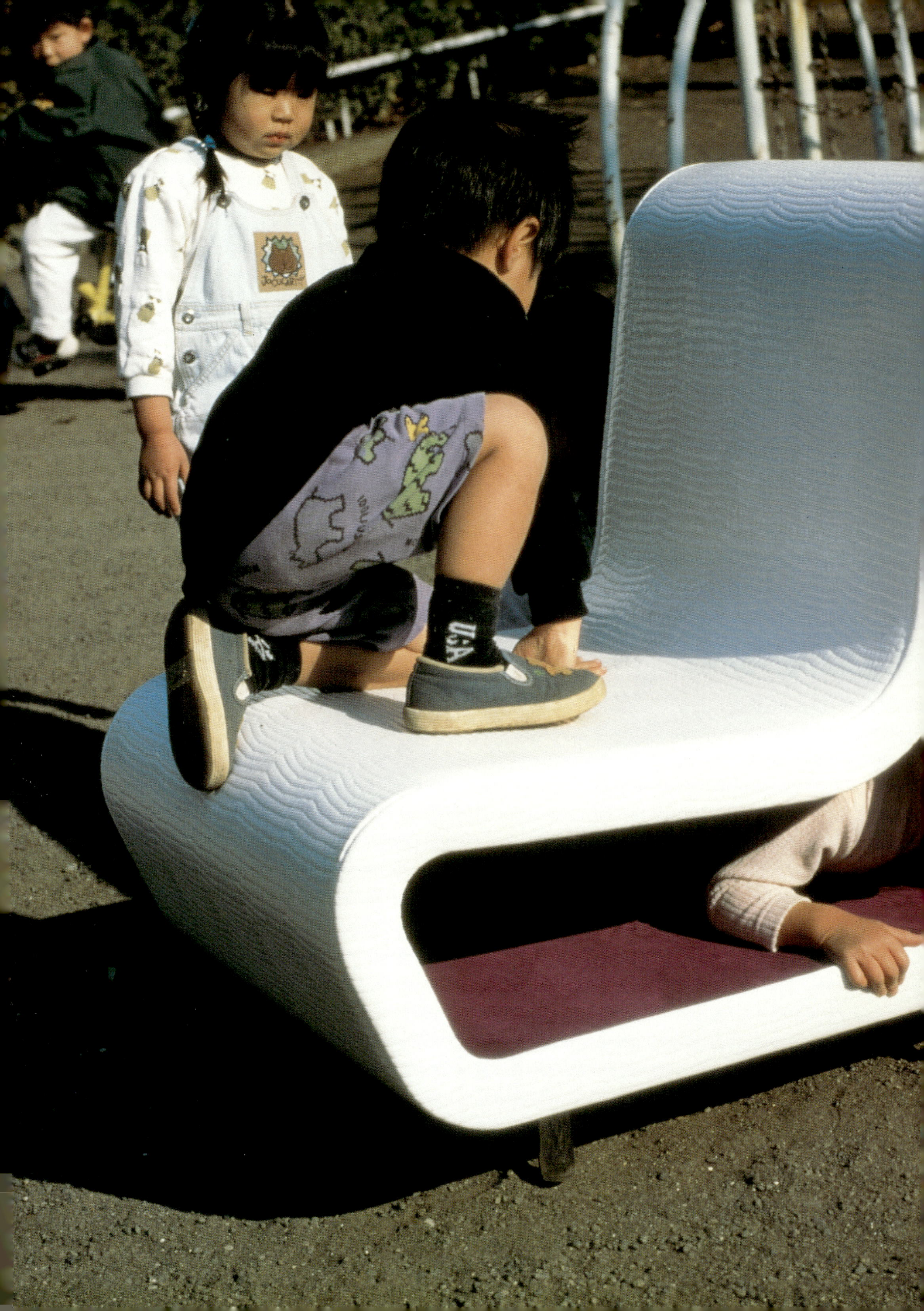
U.S.A

奉納

'We try to make things that everyone can enjoy. We don't want to be elitist, and our approach is far from academic. Architecture is all about the visual; you never find a note inside that describes the concept'

A project that 'speaks for itself' – that's the catch phrase at KDa. 'Years ago, when we couldn't explain our ideas in proper Japanese, we used drawings and sketches. We gesticulated.' Mark grins at the memory. 'It's that sort of visual communication which is still so essential to our work.'

A flair for trends and fashions sometimes appears in their work as a retro look – a flashback to the '60s and '70s. They often opt for the most obvious solution, like the artificial trees and other forest-related objects that characterise KDa's design for the La Foret Building. Some critics may consider their unambiguous approach superficial, but others, like myself, label it light-hearted and unpretentious.

Given the Japanese thirst for novelty, the team knows that anything new goes down really well. This applies to architecture and to anything else under the rising sun. The La Foret project boasted a world premiere: a wall of optical fibres. Despite the sky-high cost of installation – countered to some extent by the low cost of maintenance – the client loved the idea of being identified with something brand new.

In designing the Vrooom! garage, Klein Dytham used a new insulating paint developed by NASA. The client encouraged them to try it. But novelty alone isn't the main criterion. 'We want each design to suit the particular project involved,' Astrid explains. 'Our goal is a design that responds well to the brief, doesn't exceed the budget and respects the allotted time frame. We feel the same about materials. We try to use them in a relevant way, to let them express their special qualities. Take this new artificial wood developed by a housing builder. It looks incredibly organic. Our idea would be to use it in a way that would never work if it were natural wood, such as in a counter made of one piece, for example, with lots of curves. People would do a double take before finally realising that it's fake wood.' Humour, technology, colour and materials are all key elements of KDa's work.

Another strong point is a knack for promoting the name of the firm, as well as that of the collective. Although Klein and Dytham certainly can't be pigeonholed as 'architects to the core', they're quick to point out that their peripheral

49   >> 57

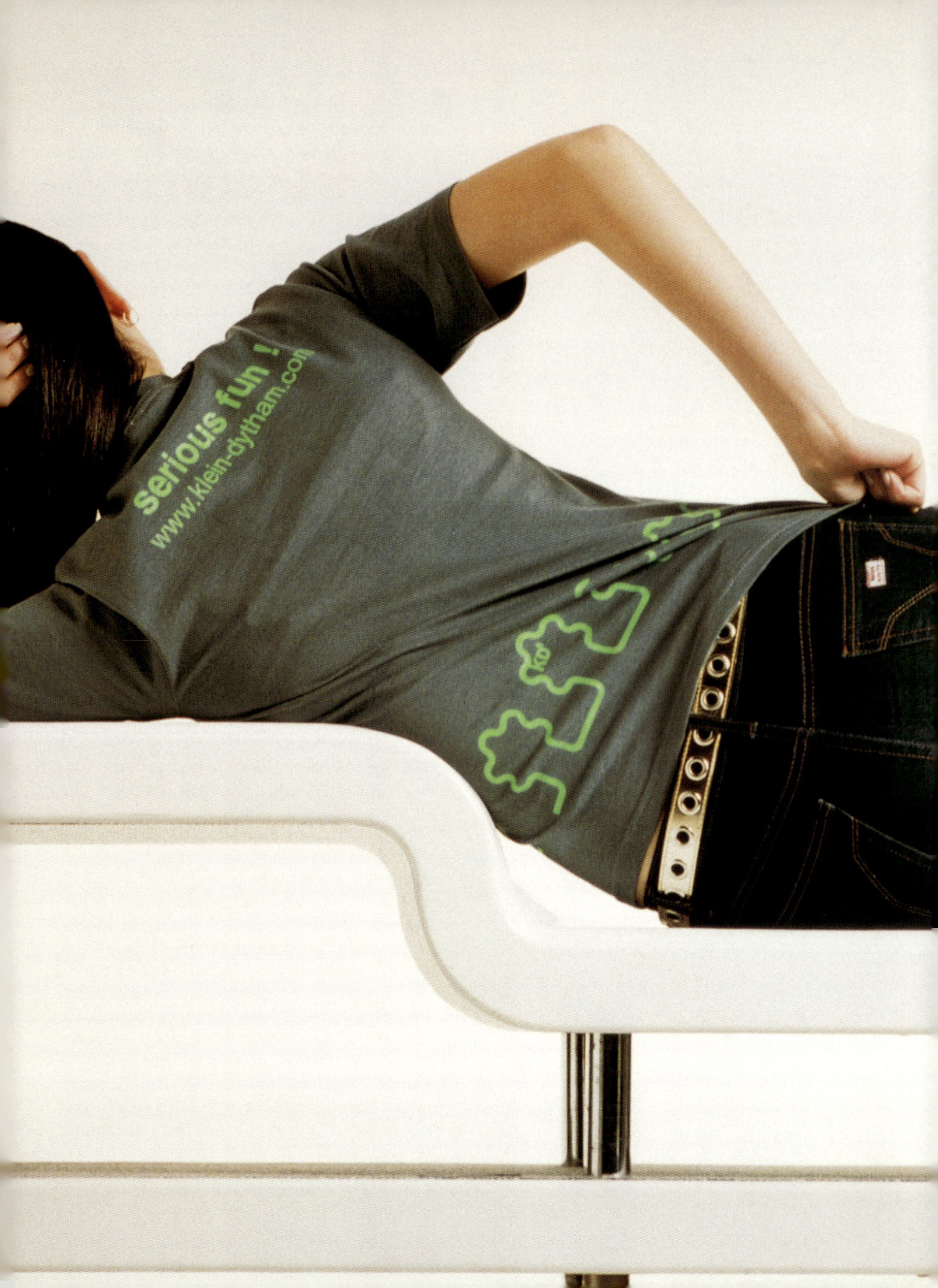
serious fun !
www.klein-dytham.com

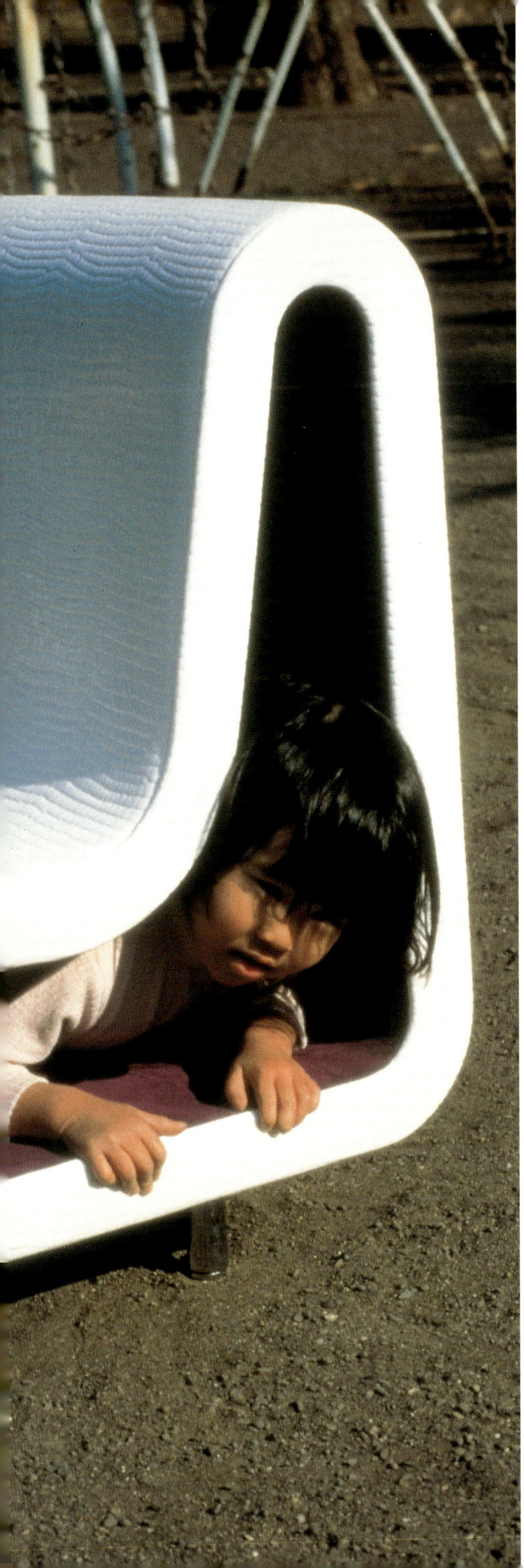

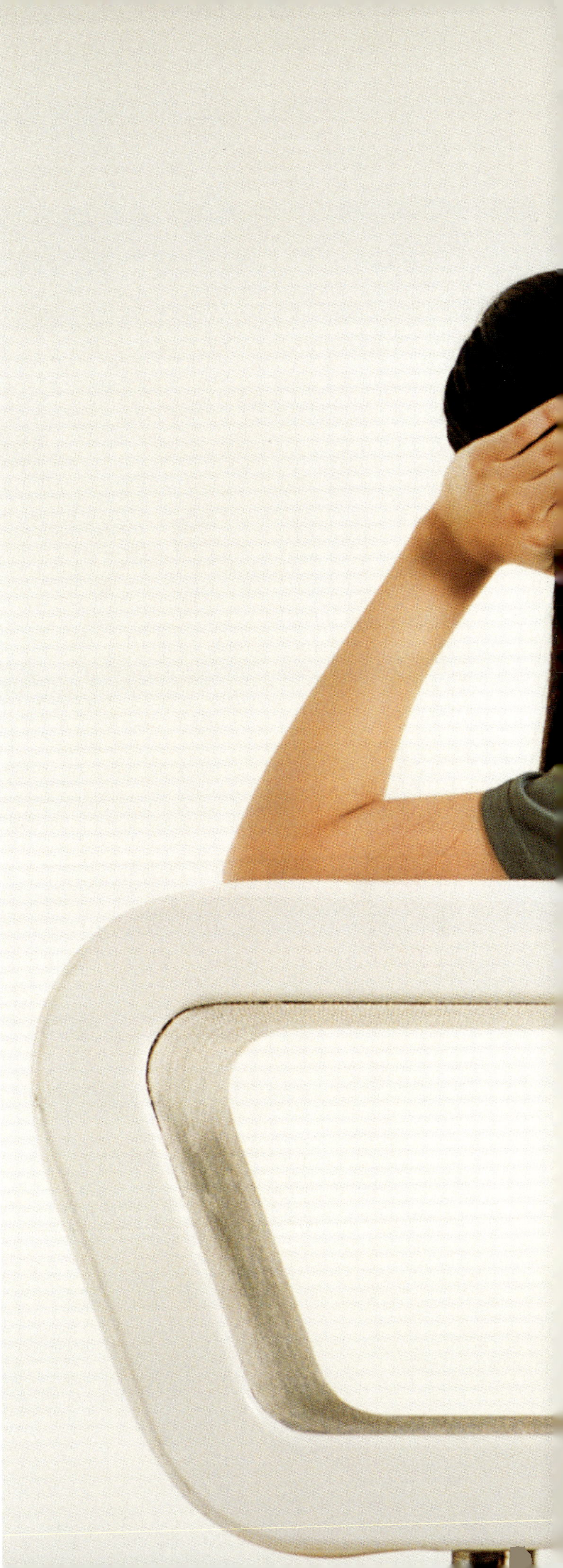

Chu-Coo Chair and Bench (2)

Model: Miss Universe Japan 2001, Misao Arauchi (1981)

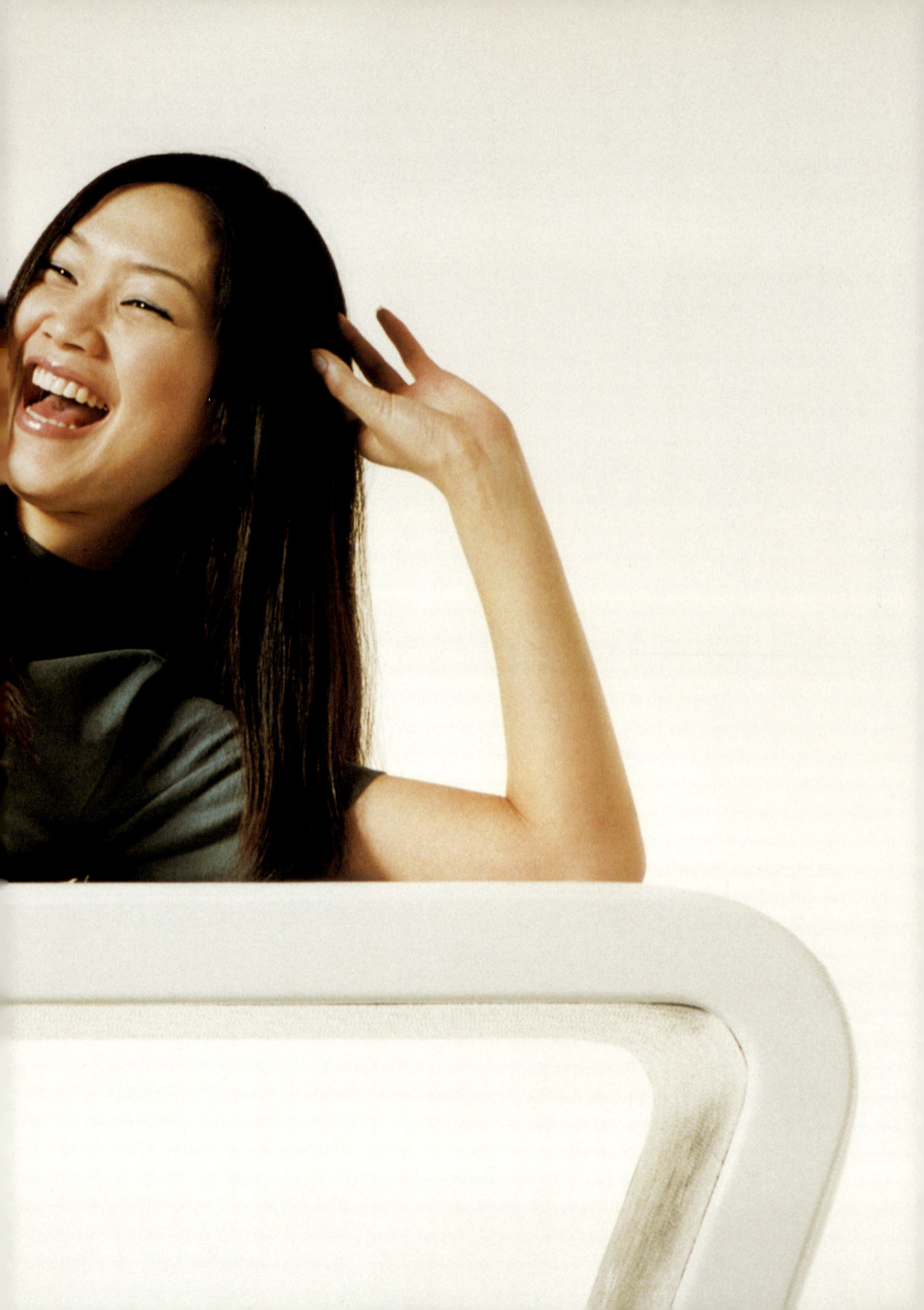

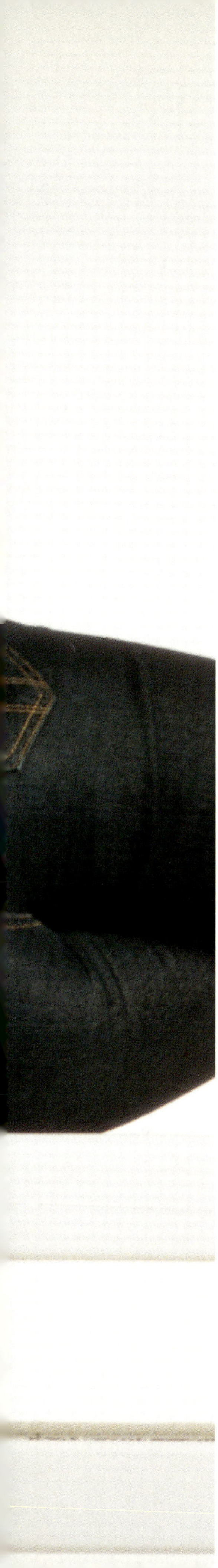
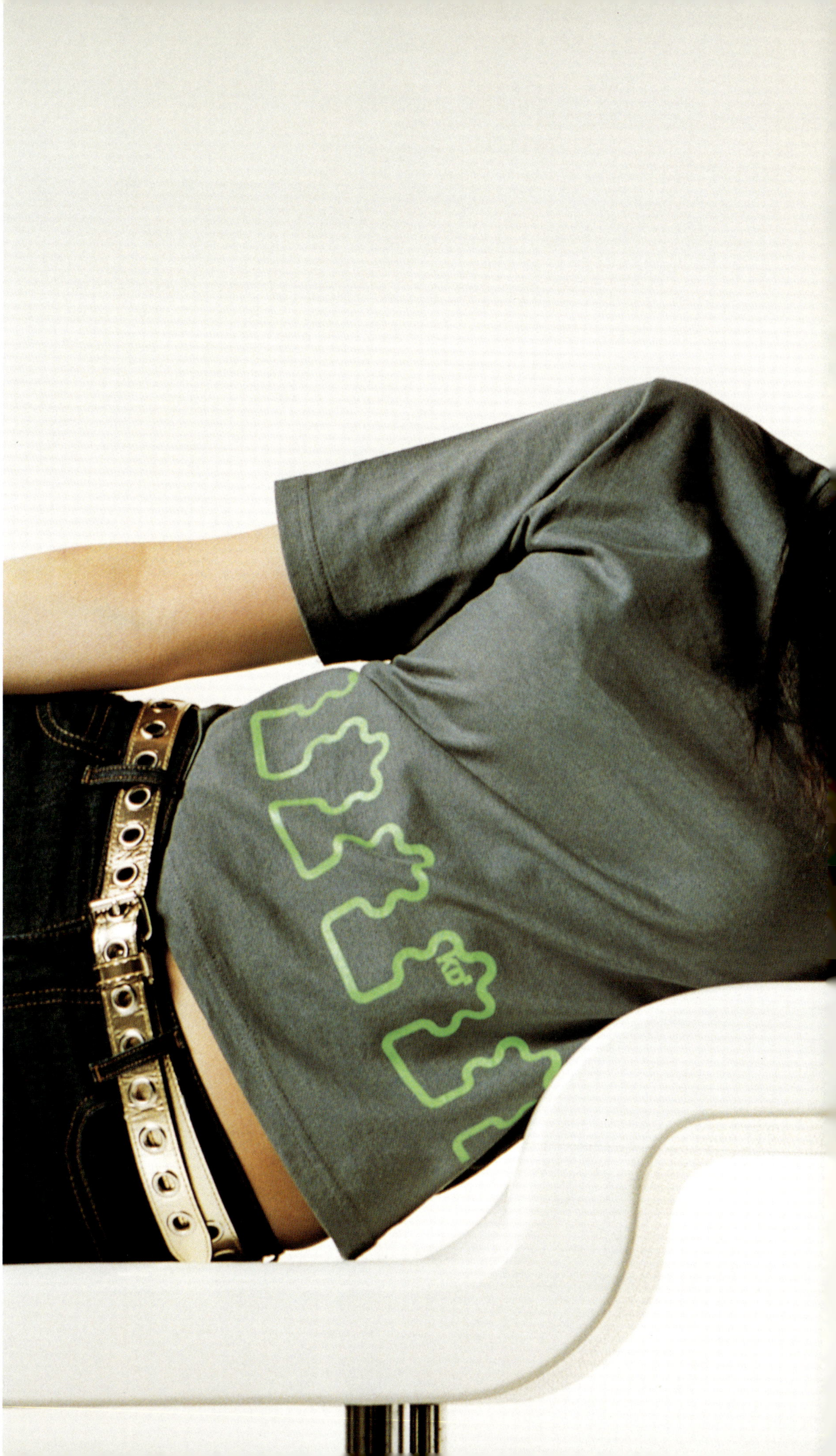

Some critics may consider their unambiguous approach superficial, but others label it light-hearted and unpretentious activities are 'mostly for fun'. Nevertheless, brewing beer and organising art-related events are part of building a widespread public image as a creative team par excellence. Clients have come to think of them not simply as the umpteenth architecture firm to set up shop in Tokyo, but as a smart, exciting group of people that get things done.

With no official policy on the appearance of buildings, Tokyo presents a bewildering array of modern architecture, a cityscape rich in diversity and visual discord. 'When you're a young architect, dying to do wild projects, Tokyo is the perfect city,' Astrid laughs. 'Just follow the building regulations, and your design can look like anything you want it to.'

Mark finds the city inspiring. 'There's a lack of context. Whatever you see today may be knocked down by next year. Everything is more or less disposable, and change is inevitable. It's a refreshing way to look at architecture.' This train of thought leads him to convenience stores, which 'can't leave anything as it is. It's all about improvement, about creating a new look. Change the chocolate bar, renew the beer can, buy the latest mobile phone.'

The English, he claims, want to keep things for life. 'Think of Burberry and of all those classic items made of leather. Guys use their leather briefcases forever — they love the idea. From the perspective of architecture, bricks get better as they age. Maybe because so many ancient European structures still exist, Europeans want products that will last just as long.' Not so in Japan, where the average building is only 25 years old at the time of its demolition and subsequent replacement.

'The demand for new things does keep us on our toes,' Astrid remarks. 'We can't be seen turning out the same old recipe. Our clients want innovative designs, which means we have to reinvent ourselves as well. A fresh face and a different approach to analysing the latest project can result in that unique — and uniquely relevant — solution that we're always waiting to discover.'

Carolien van Tilburg is a Dutch journalist and media producer who has lived in Japan since 1995. Thanks to an avid interest in the fields of architecture and design, she has become a regular contributor to Frame.

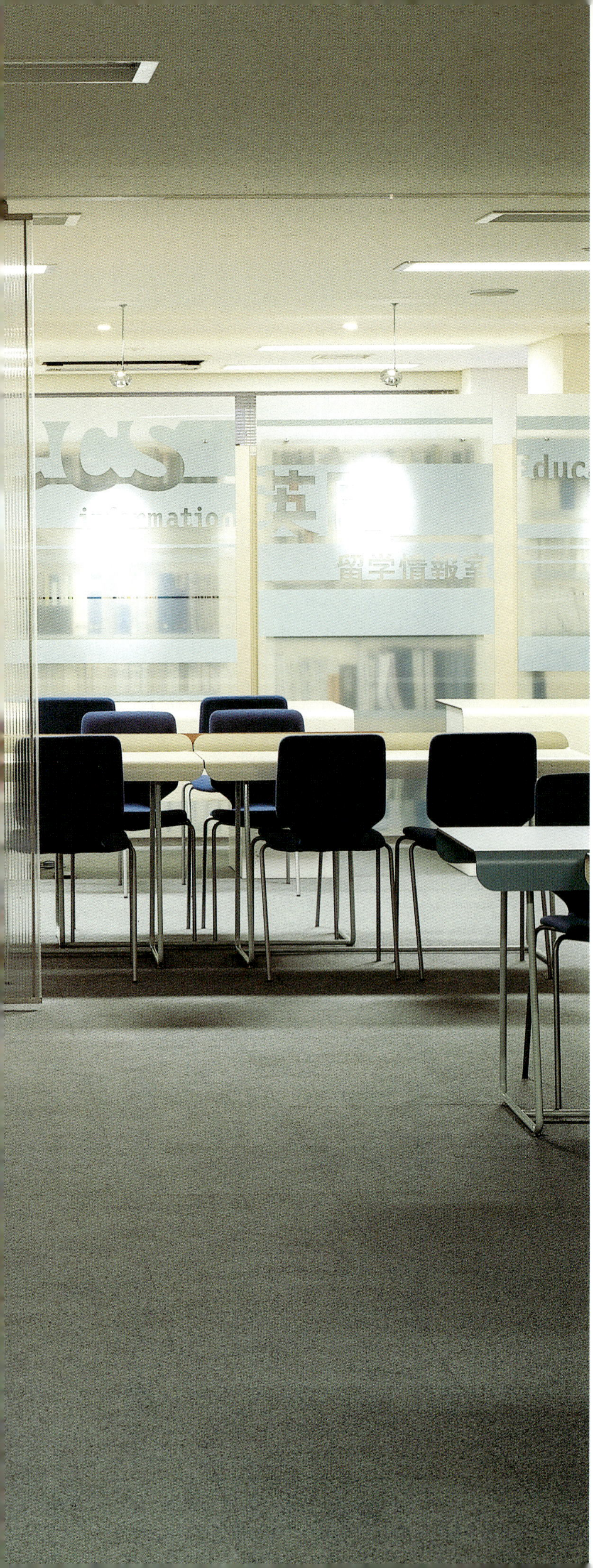

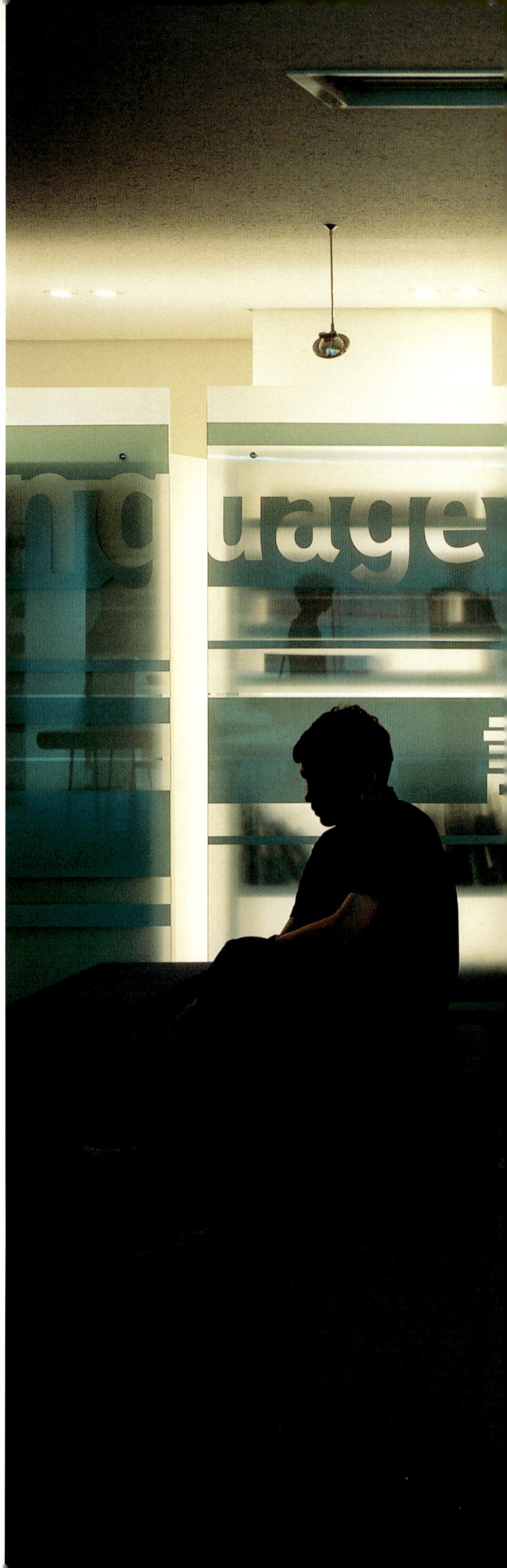

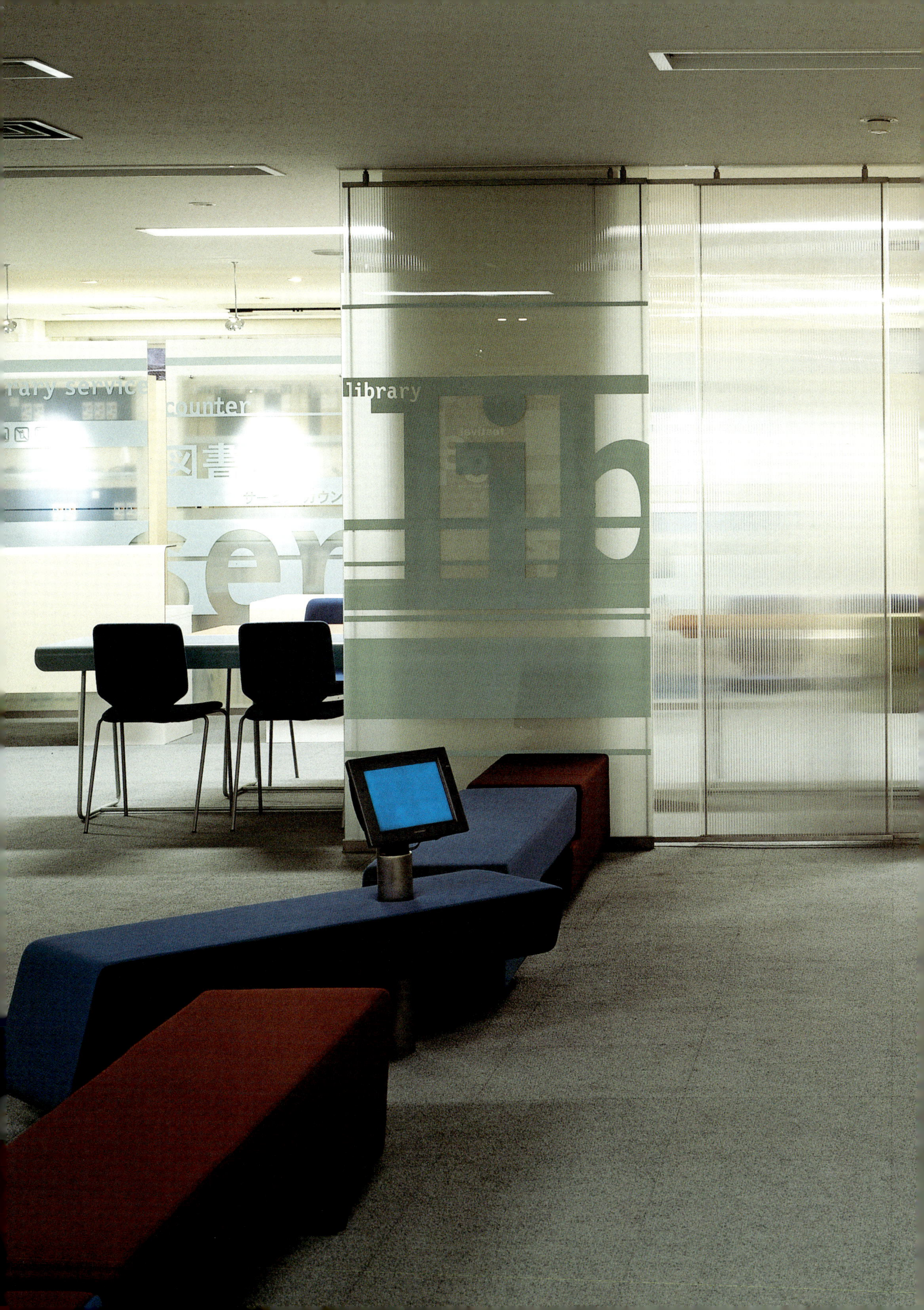
library
lib
counter
図書

British Council Information Centre

In anticipation of the digital technologies that will transform most libraries in the future, KDa accorded the books a literally peripheral role in this design. The opaque glass screens give the books a somewhat mystique aura, moving them 'out of focus' and making space for a lively information hub in the centre. The cloister ambience is emphasised by warm lighting around the edges, while cool light illuminates the central space to facilitate screen-based activities using computers, videos, and satellite broadcast technology. Large bilingual graphics on the glass screens indicate different areas of interest.

The design required careful organisation of the building's various zones to accommodate the library and adjacent information lounge as well as a counselling centre for English studies. As the various sections have different opening hours, benches are used to block off those areas closed to the public. Arranged in a straight line, they form a partition that shuts off one of the facilities. The lighting is dimmed in the area not in use. When open, visitors can rotate the seats to watch BBC World Service comfortably. Screens are mounted on the benches.

The colours are an interesting combination of serious navy blue and reddish brown with vivid pale blue and green. At the front is an information lounge with comfortable sofas. People pop in and out, find the information they need, read a periodical, have a conversation, all in a very relaxing atmosphere.

Location: Kagurazaka, Shinjuku-ku, Tokyo / Client: The British Council / Graphic Design: Namaiki / General Contractor: D. Brain Co. Ltd / Start Design: February 1997 / Completion: March 1998 / Floor Area: 445 square metres / Wall: computer-cut graphics on translucent glass screen, twin-wall polycarbonate screens / Furniture: custom-made swivelling bench divider, post-formed Bakelite tabletops / Photography: Mitsumasa Fujitsuka, Nacása & Partners

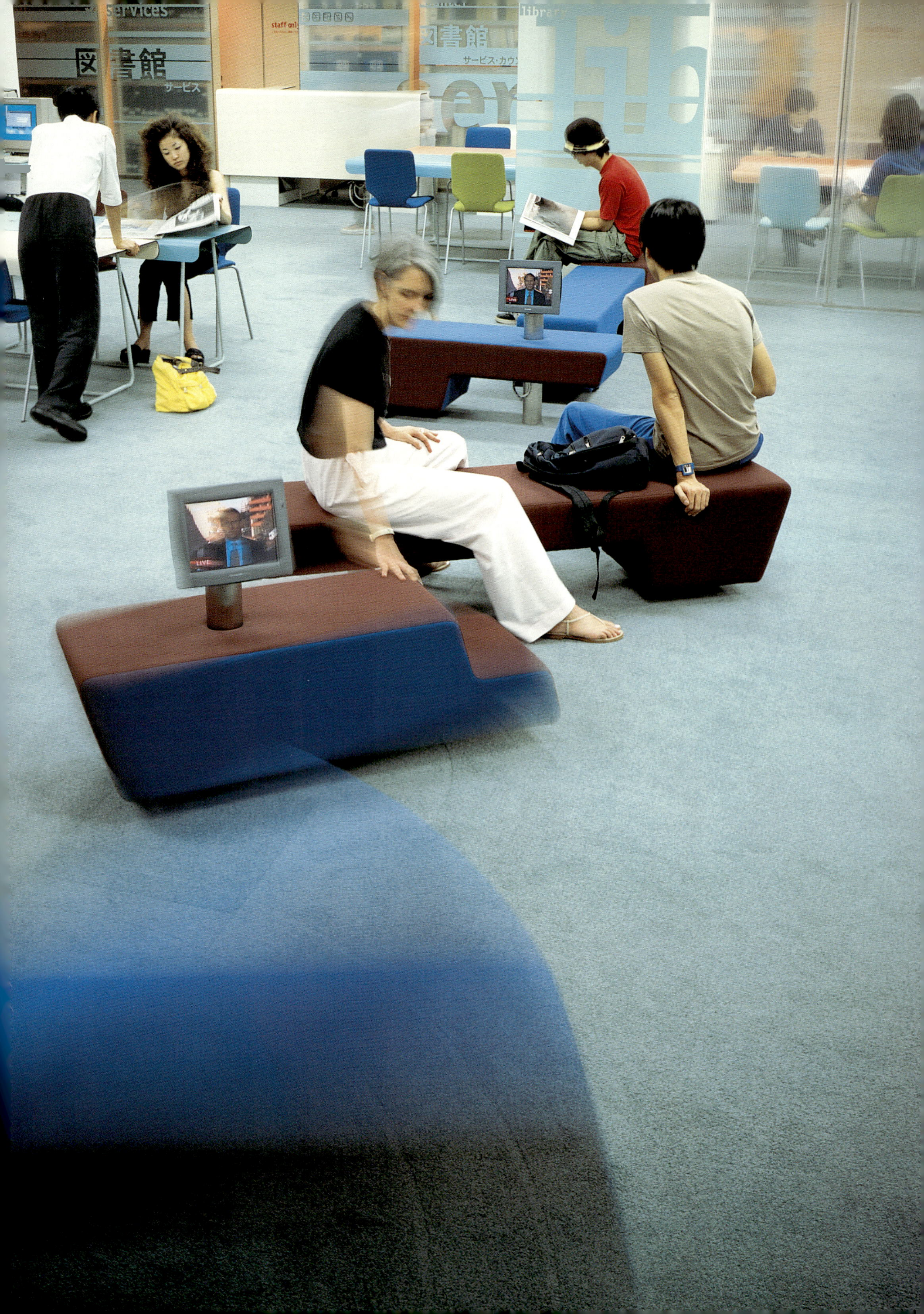

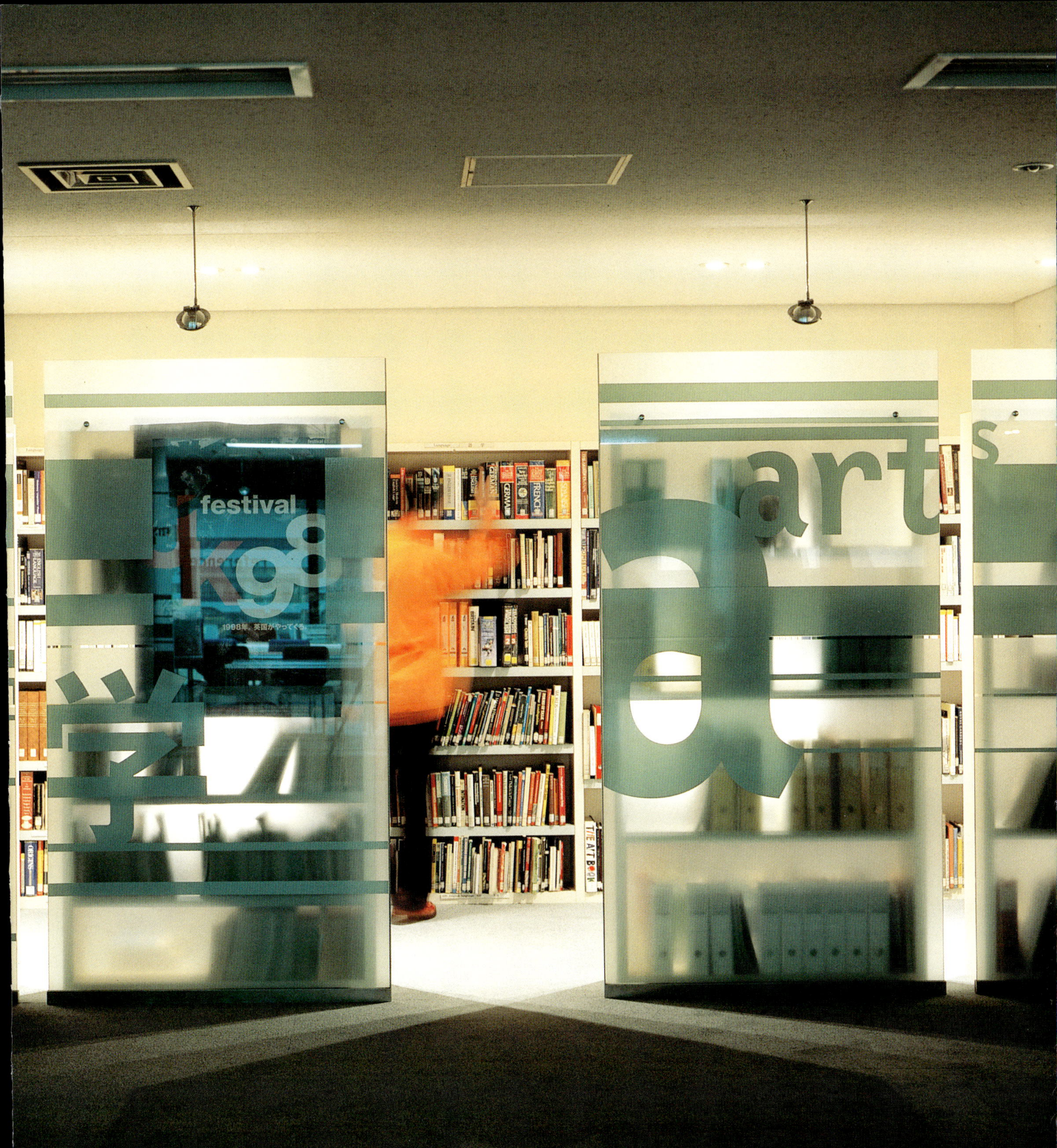
festival
arts

For all the exotic tinge that working in the city
at the end of the world brings, the practice's roots
are firmly in Europe, a culture which of course looks
just as bafflingly mysterious and exotic from
a different perspective as Japanese kitsch
and Manga comics appear from here

A Little Long-Distance Flash of Wit

It's quite hard to lose Astrid Klein and Mark Dytham's telephone number, if only because they are so good at reminding you. Every year their Christmas card arrives. It's always stylish, and it's always ingenious. One year it's an inflatable, the next it comes with a built-in music chip. Every time the card arrives it brings with it a little long-distance flash of wit, reflecting their unusual ability to combine London's scavenging instincts with Tokyo's technological abundance. Either way, you don't throw it away in a hurry.

But the last time I went to Japan I had somehow managed to lose track of the current number, so I tried the web site instead. The first thing I saw was an image of Mark photographed outside Buckingham Palace in a morning suit complete with tails, striped trousers and top hat, holding up the medal for services to British architecture that the Queen had just pinned onto his coat. It was a reminder that for all the exotic tinge that working in the city at the end of the world as one critic me memorably described Tokyo brings, the practice's roots are firmly in Europe, a culture which of course looks just as bafflingly mysterious and exotic from a different perspective as Japanese kitsch and Manga comics appear from here. And that there is a strong streak of Englishness to Klein Dytham's work. In England, at the time they were being educated, architecture was dominated by the idea of High Tech, a kind of nostalgia for the country's vanished manufacturing traditions, which has infected the imagination of a certain strand of its designers ever since. An infection made manifest in its passion for Meccano construction toys, and for the aesthetic qualities of steam engines, World War Two bombers and Jeeps. In Britain's post-industrial condition it encouraged architects to try to create buildings that looked like the product of the most advanced industrial technology, but which were actually made by hand. At its most impressive, it's the culture of hand-made fibreglass and extruded aluminium racing yachts, or one-off Formula One racing cars at which Britain still excels, and it depends on ingenuity rather than relying on the capacity of local industrial manufacturing skills.

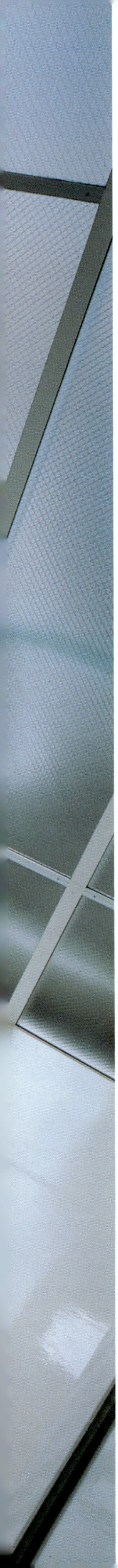

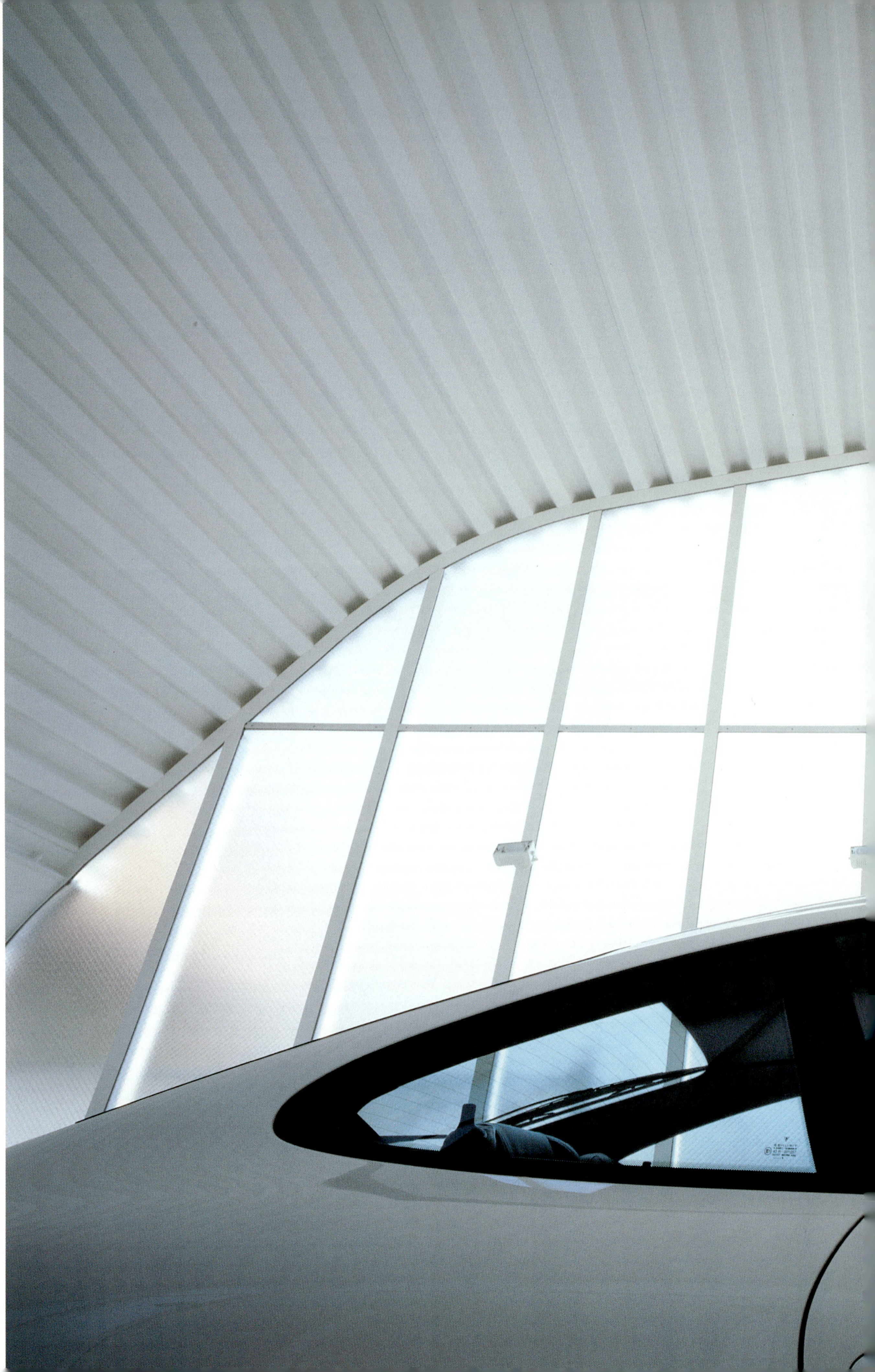

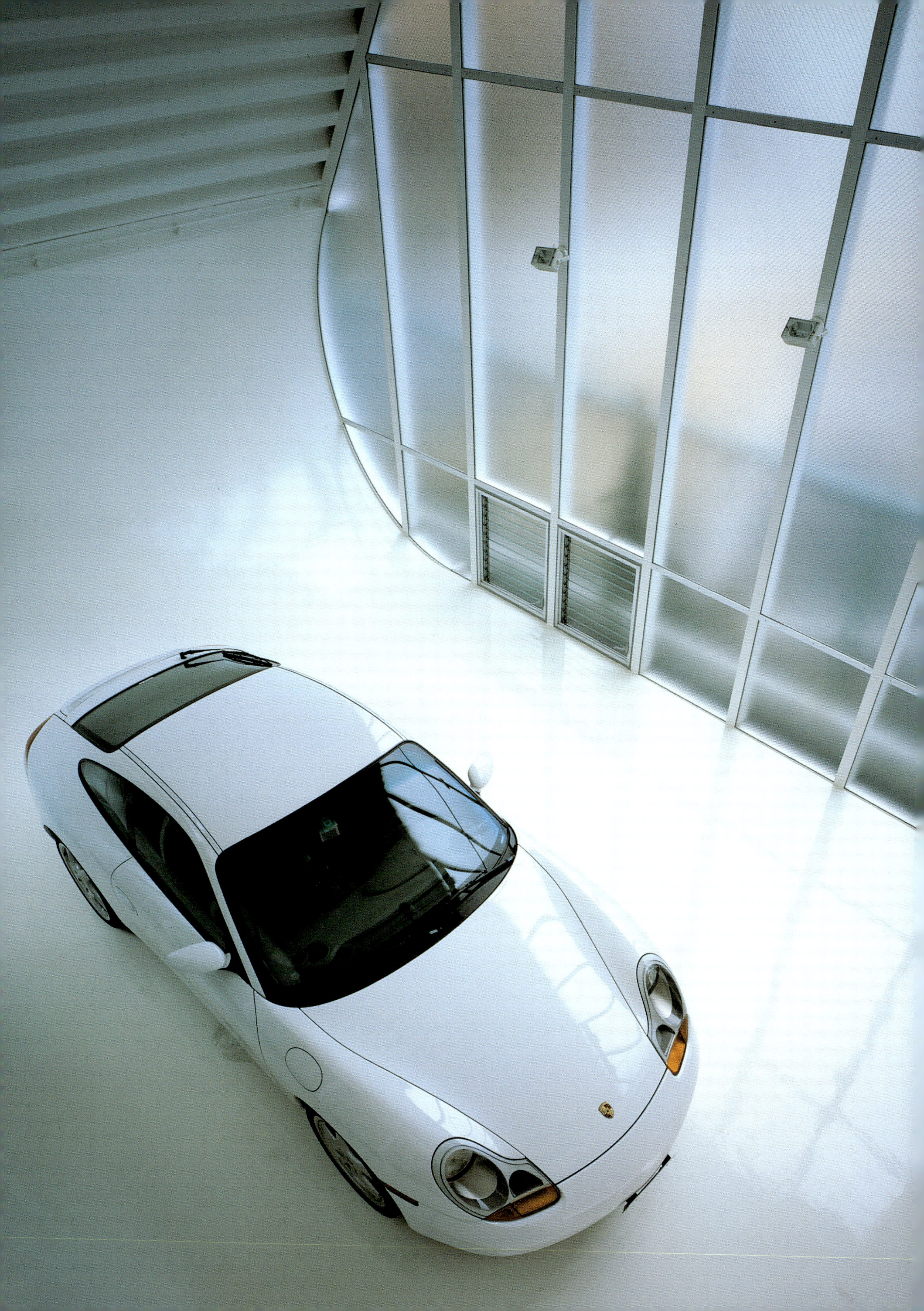

Vrooom! (1)

The client, an avid car enthusiast, asked KDa to design a garage for his collection of Italian and his wife's German cars. The challenge was to house six stunningly beautiful cars on a long and narrow site, and incorporate a study and viewing area on an upper level. Conceived as one continuous surface, the garage floor sweeps up to form the roof, framing the cars as if in a photo studio and creating a flowing aerodynamic shape. Window mullions act as slender columns that support the roof, similar to the way a car roof rests on metal uprights between windscreens and side windows. The profiled steel roof structure functions as both roof slab and stiffening membrane. The space is intentionally neutral so that attention is focused on the cars. Up-lighters directed towards the ceiling provide an indirect source of lighting for the cars, avoiding any pin spots or glare from direct illumination.

Since only sixty per cent of the site could be built on, the remaining forty per cent is covered by a convertible roof that takes the car analogy even further. When completely open, one section of the retractable roof is in a vertical position and doubles the height of the façade to the street. This vertical leaf forms a screen preventing direct views from neighbouring properties into the study area.

Location: Aichi prefecture / General Contractor: Ukai - Gumi / Structural Engineer: Structured Environment / Mechanical Engineer: Heartland Engineering / Start Design: January 1999 / Completion: September 1999 / Floor Area: 118 square metres / Structure: reinforced concrete, steel frame / Floor: epoxy resin on concrete / Wall: frosted wired glass / Shutter: profiled aluminium sheet on aluminium frame / Ceiling: profiled steel roof, convertible aluminium roof / Photography: Kozo Takayama

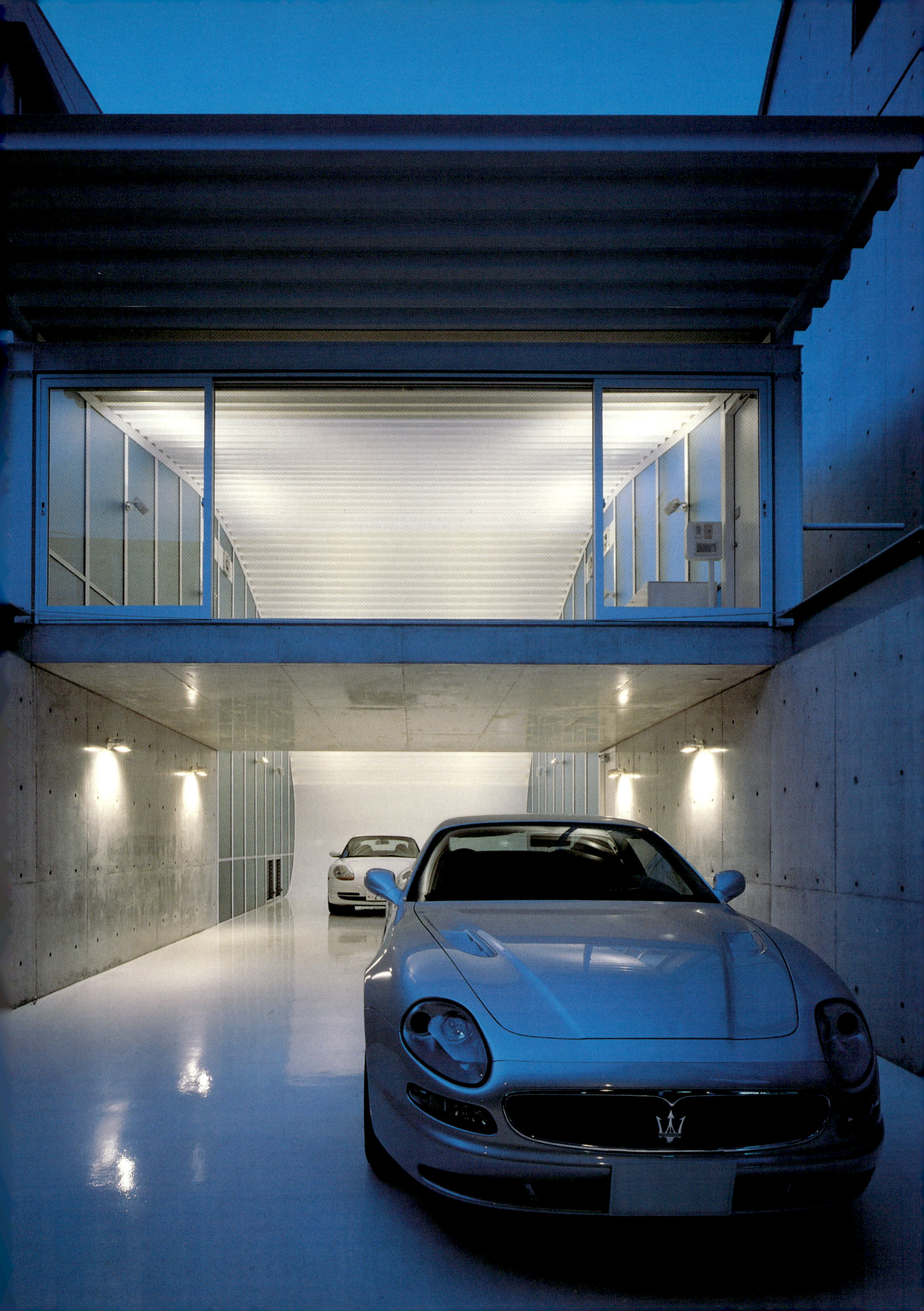

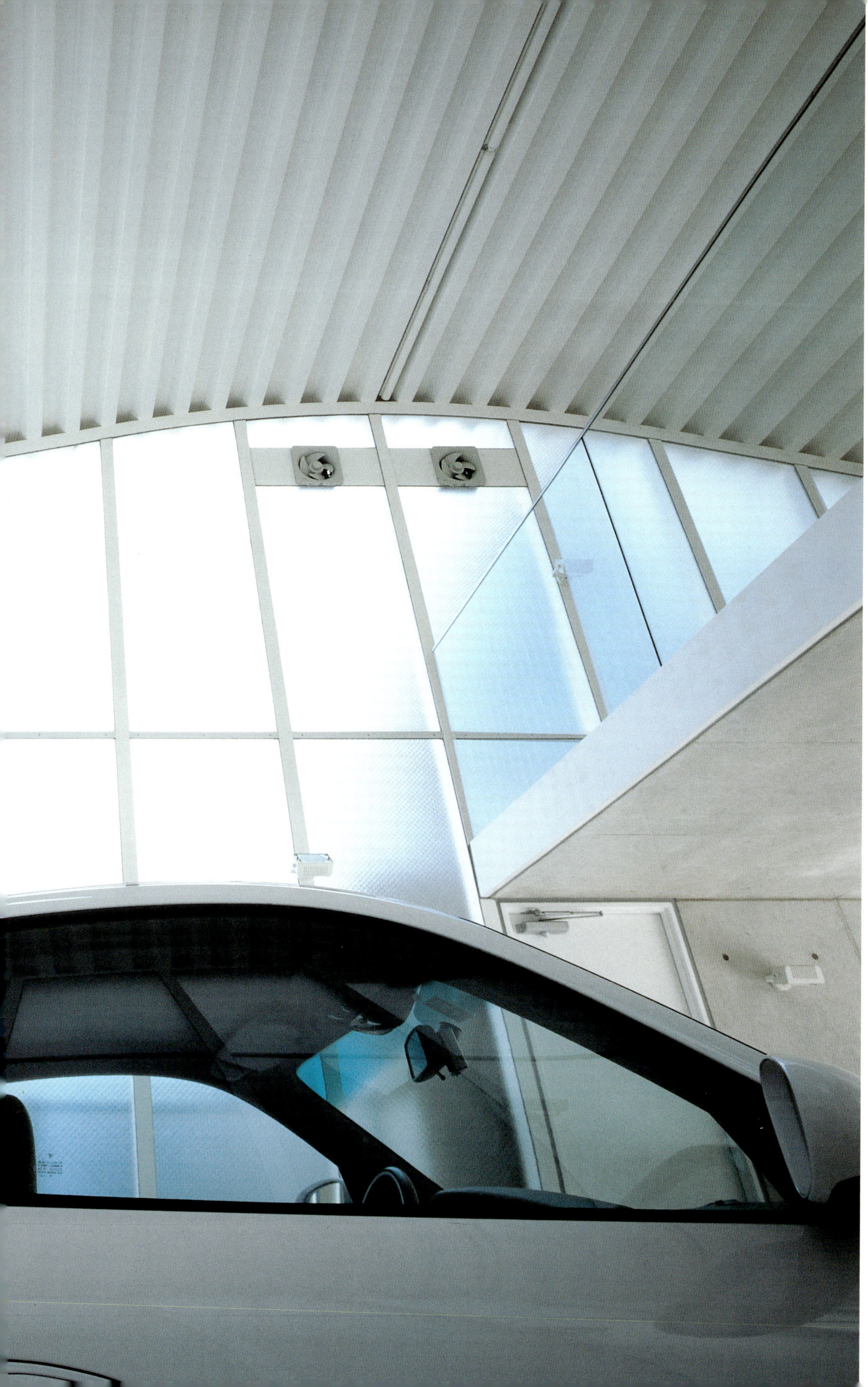

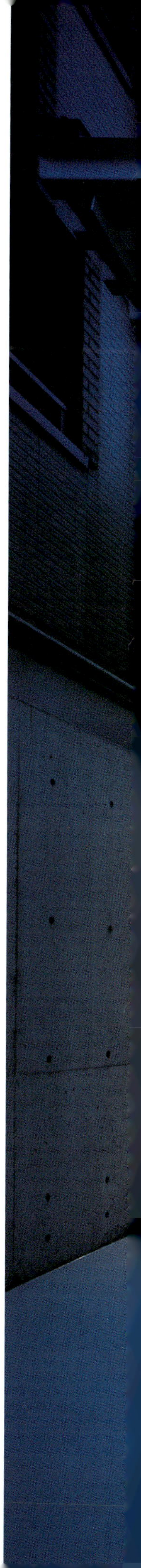

Dytham and Klein are exploring a fascinating marginal territory, somewhere between London and Tokyo, and between architecture and design

Dytham and Klein are not, it seems to me, ideologically driven toward architecture, nor do they approach it as high culture. Rather they are exploring a fascinating marginal territory, somewhere between London and Tokyo, and between architecture and design. They make ephemeral events rather than buildings. Operating in such a situation their first instinct is to be engaging. They have understood that to make things that do not last memorable they must depend more than anything on the quality of their ideas and their imagination rather than hiding behind alibis.

The two of them arrived in Tokyo just after the bubble of the boom years had well and truly burst. And as a result they have had a very different experience of Japan from the somewhat hallucinogenic world of excess that the first generation of European architects who worked there in the early 1980s encountered. In those days a mysterious fax arriving in the middle of the night could be enough to catapult bright young things from the squalor of their London garret into nebulously defined multi-million-dollar projects fuelled by massively inflated Japanese property values, characterised by mutual incomprehension between Japanese and European sides of the transaction, and whose only requirement was to be more conspicuous, more wilfully extreme than the competition.

Dytham and Klein, in sharp contrast to the years of excess and first-class plane tickets, arrived in Japan with nothing more than a portfolio, at a time when Tokyo was having to deal with a sudden outbreak of reality. Exponential growth in land values had come to a sickening halt, and Japanese architecture and design had suddenly to deal with a situation that was no longer weightless, but in which the constraints familiar in the rest of the world once more applied.

The make-do-and-mend mentality of London, a city whose designers spent the 1980s struggling to survive, turned out to be the ideal basis for operating in a Japan struggling to deal with the hangover that marked the end of its period of massive growth in which absolutely anything

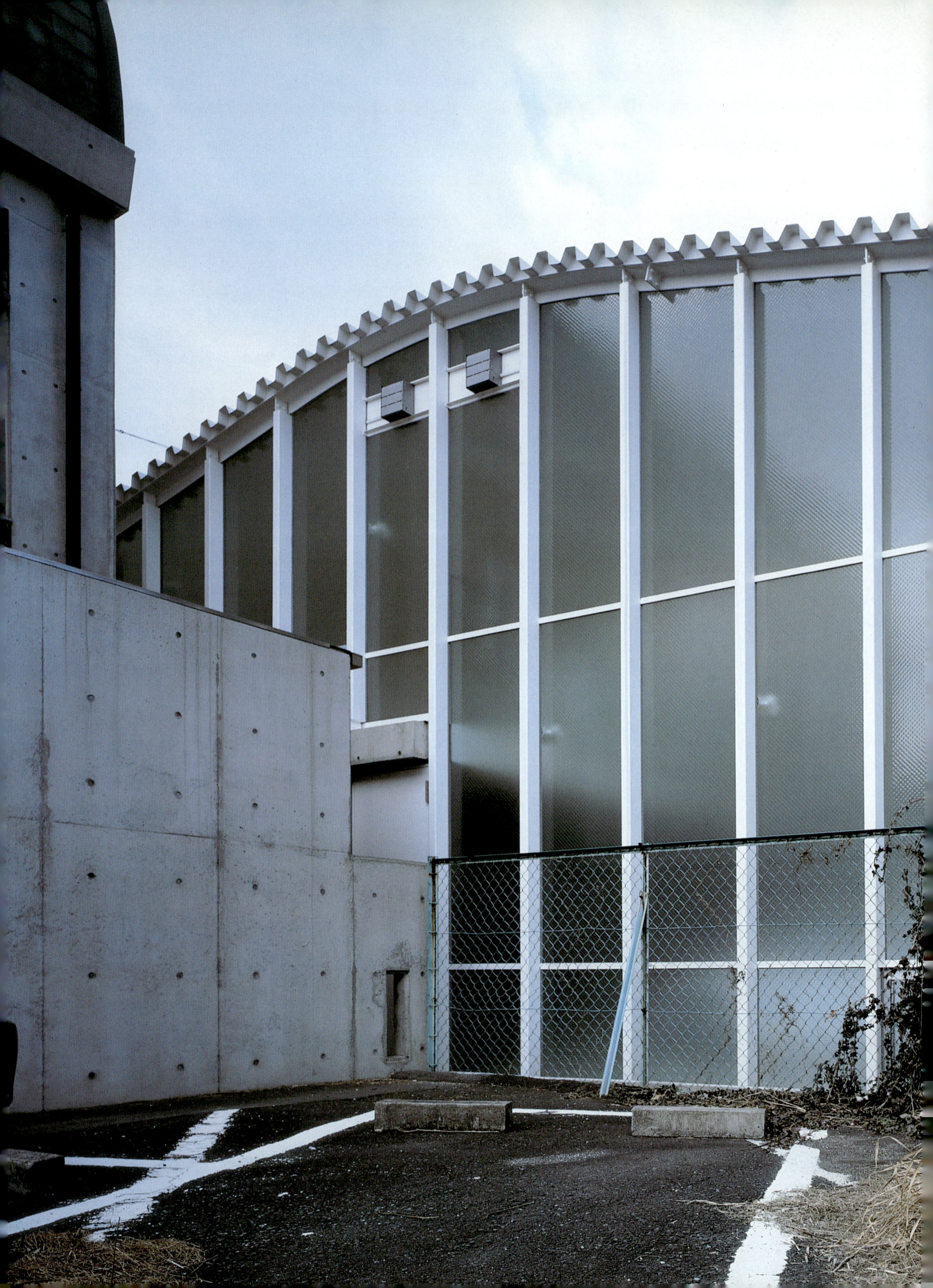

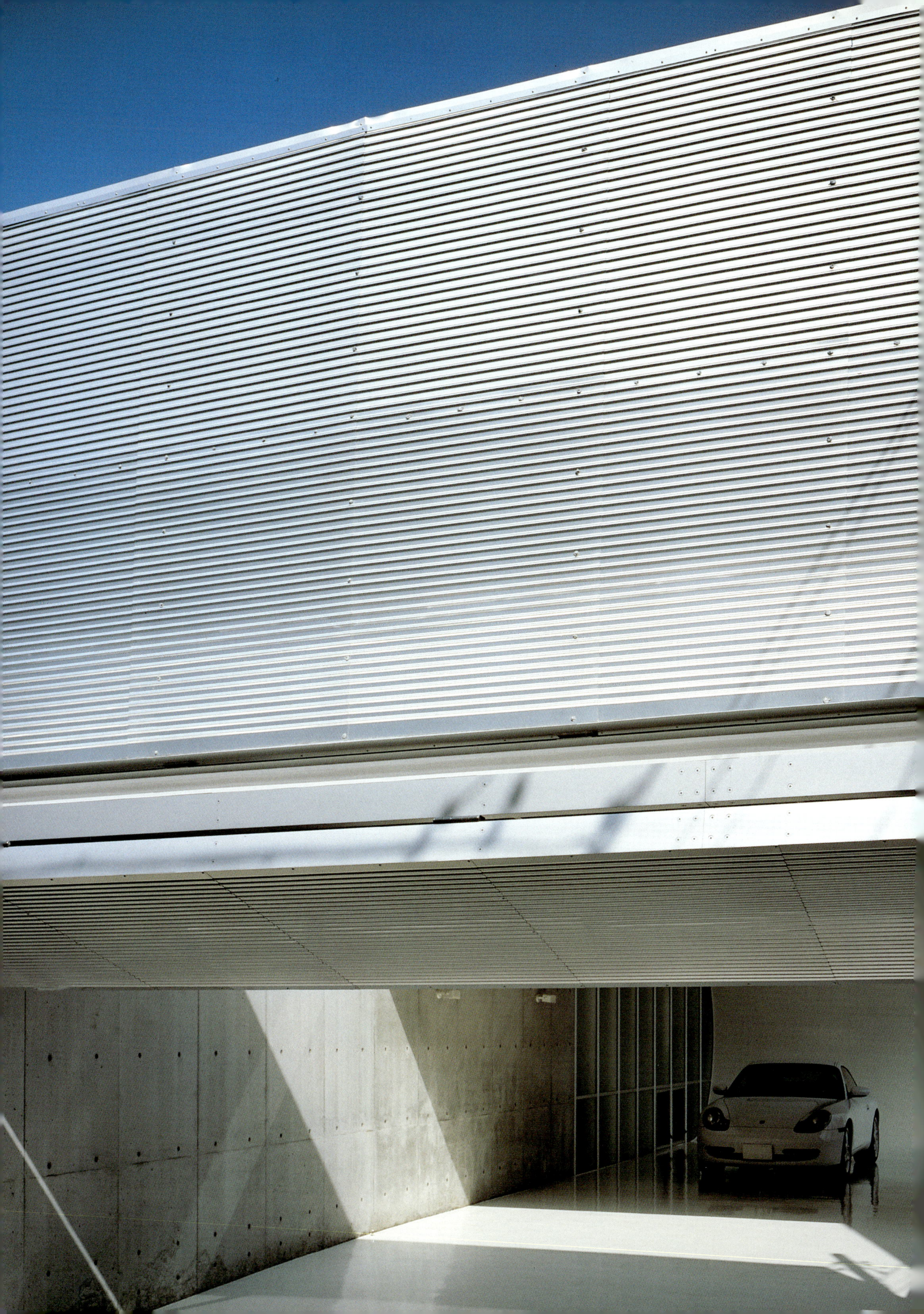

Vrooom! (2)

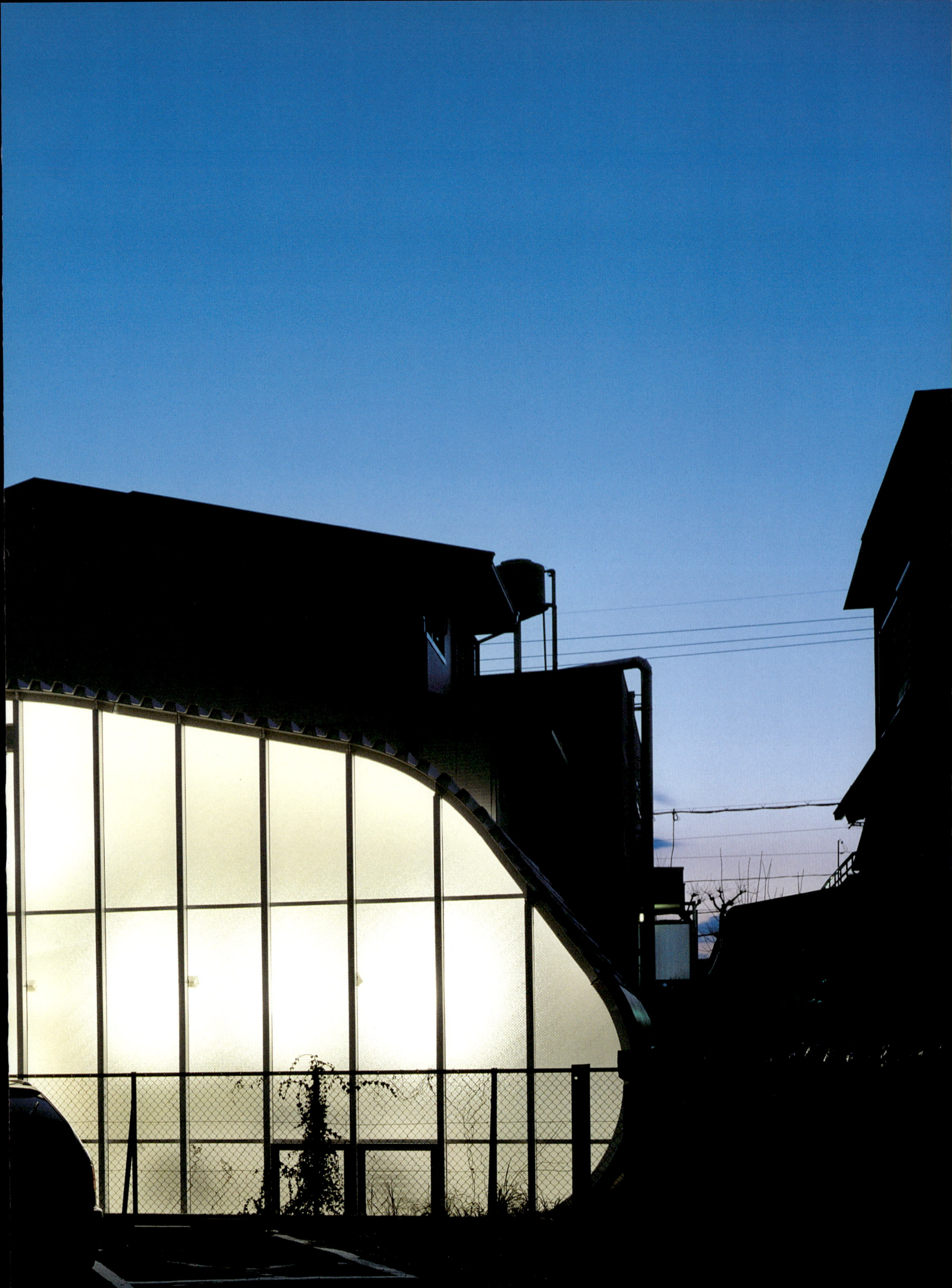

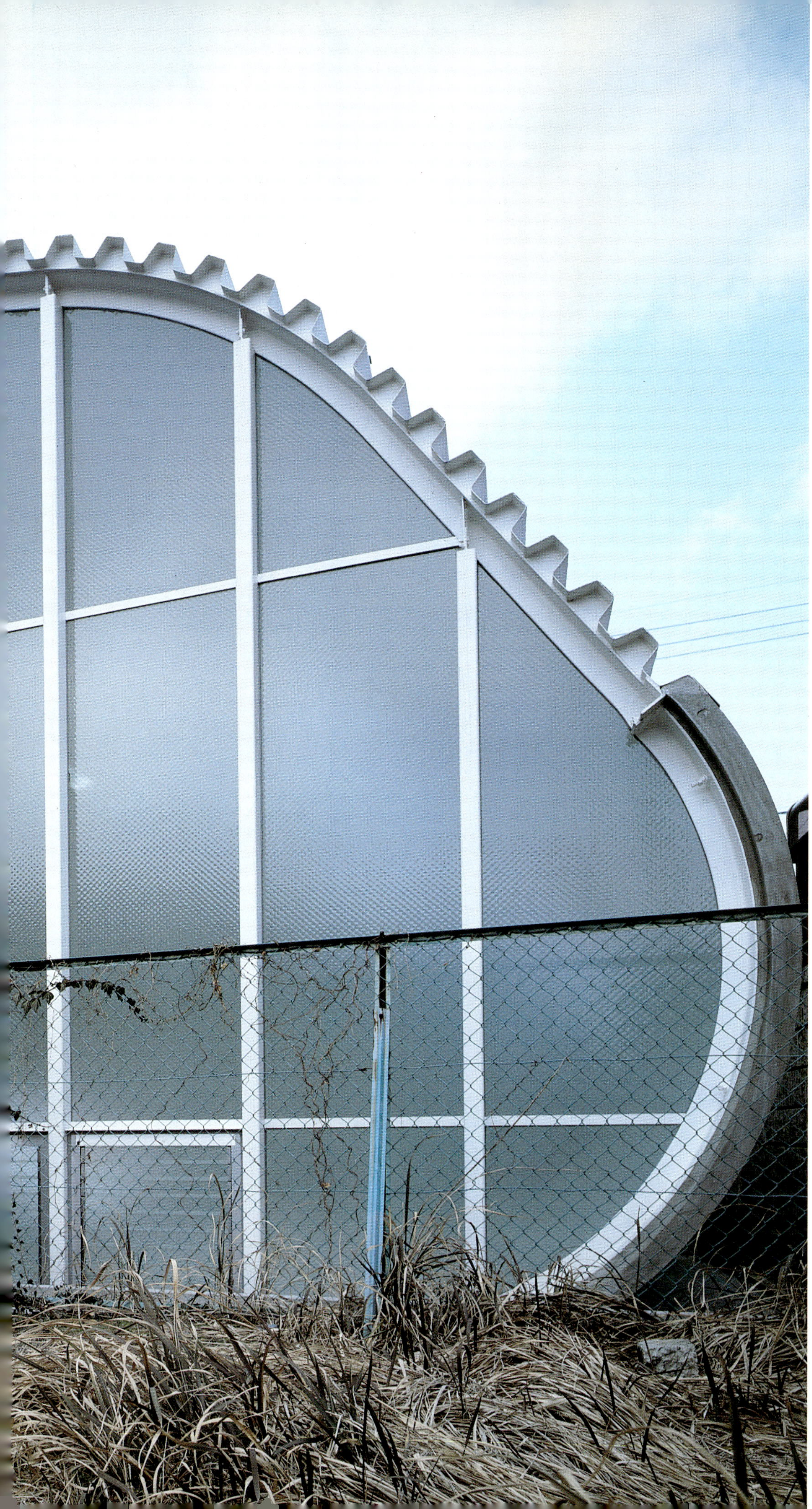
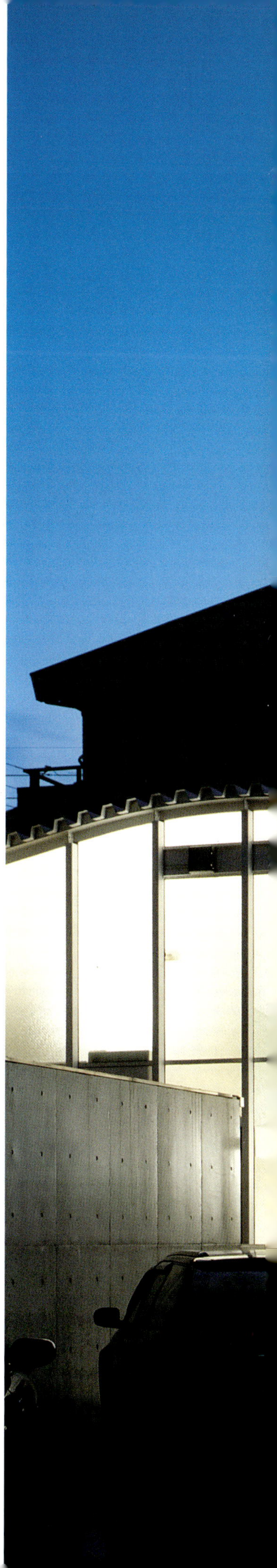

They have understood that to make things that do not last memorable they must depend more than anything on the quality of their ideas and their imagination rather than hiding behind alibis seemed to be possible. But even in this state, Tokyo is still a remarkable city, with an astonishing range of artisan skills in high-tech areas, which is still open to experiment and innovation. And it is this rich mix which has made Klein Dytham's work so continually interesting.

Deyan Sudjic graduated as an architect but chose to pursue a career as a critic, journalist and editor. In 1983 he established Blueprint, a British review of architecture and design. He has written numerous books and articles and curated several exhibitions. In 2000 he became editor-in-chief of Italian magazine Domus.

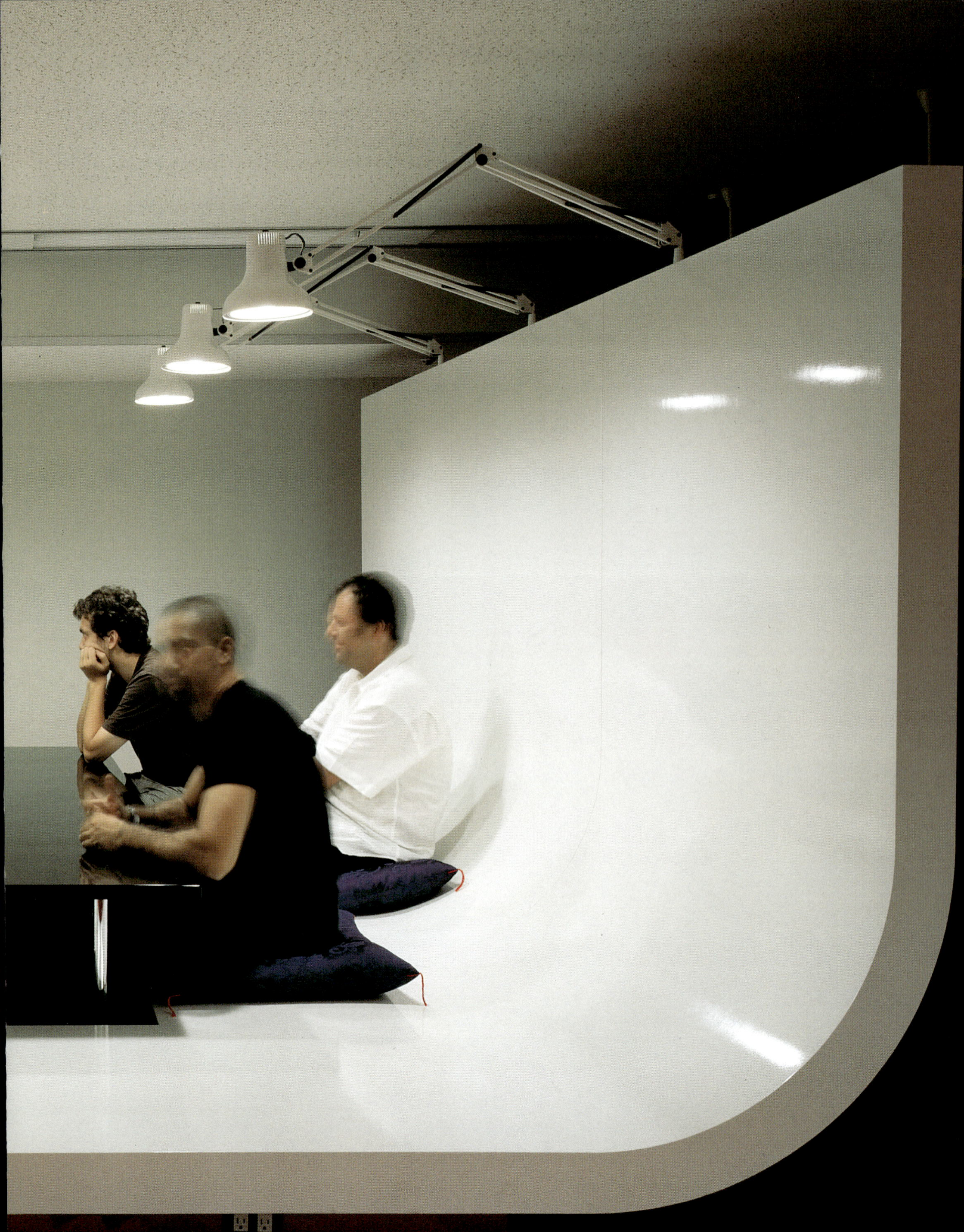

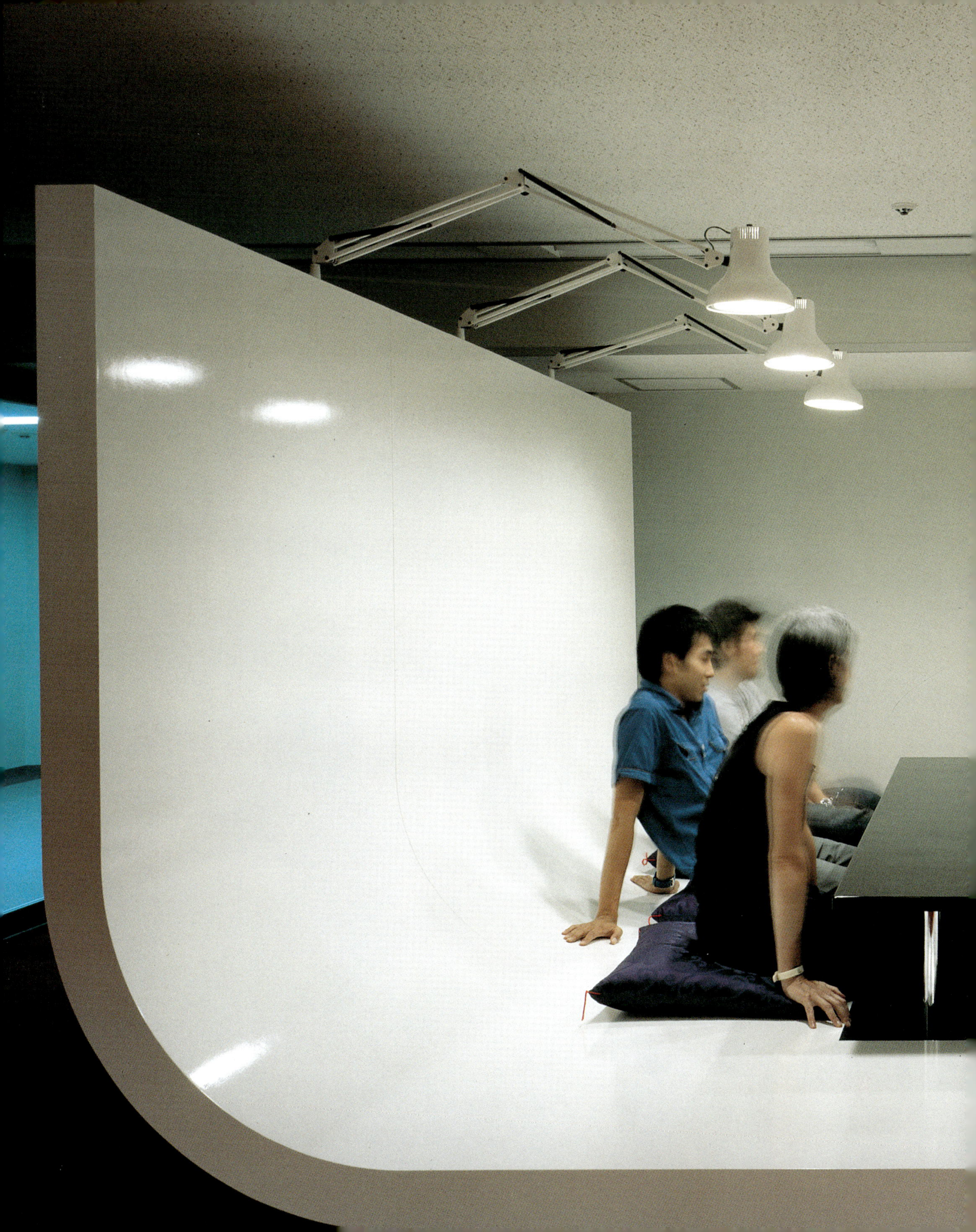

Bartle Bogle Hegarty (1)

When asked to design an office interior for the Tokyo branch of advertising agency Bartle Bogle Hegarty (BBH), KDa approached the project as though it were a piece of furniture. BBH wanted a distinctive interior with a Japanese touch but had to respect the strict requirements set down by the building's owner: no paint, nails or anything else was permitted on the walls, ceilings or floors. With a possibility that BBH might move into larger premises within a year or two, KDa designed portable installations for the interior. All components were built off site, delivered to the premises and assembled on site.

Four permanent employees work at two long, shiny, white tables, the short ends of which are rounded. Since it is possible to sit at both sides of the tables, temporary staff from the firm's headquarters in England can also work there. Those who don't require table space can sit on one of the brightly coloured Chu-Coo chairs. A row of black filing cabinets creates a sharp contrast with the many white objects in the office.

The eye-catcher, however, is the furniture piece that defines the meeting space: a huge, shiny enclosure – as large as a small room – resting on a recessed base. The U-shape seems to hover above the bright red floor, and guests have to remove their shoes before stepping onto the elevated meeting space. This 'floating' room can accommodate eight people who sit, Japanese style, on cushions in cosy proximity around a low table. The base leaves room under the table for legs and feet – no need to sit cross-legged on the floor during discussions that can last for hours. A silver curtain ensures privacy and also facilitates darkened video or slide presentations.

Simple desk lamps are mounted above the meeting room and on the tables, allowing the ceiling and walls to remain untouched. Using elementary resources – contrasts in colour and material and one showpiece – KDa managed to creat an exceptional office environment that leaves the surrounding space totally intact.

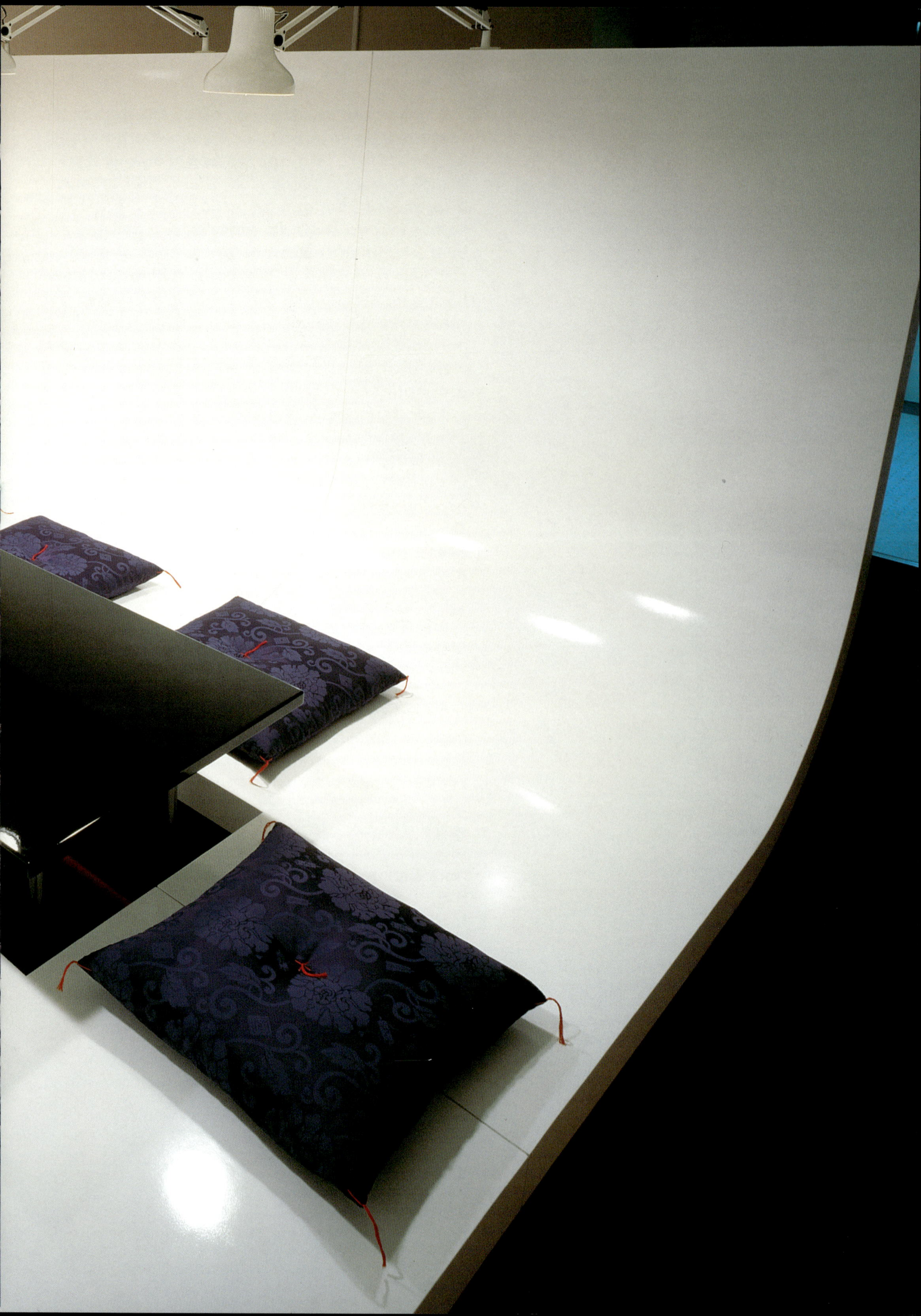

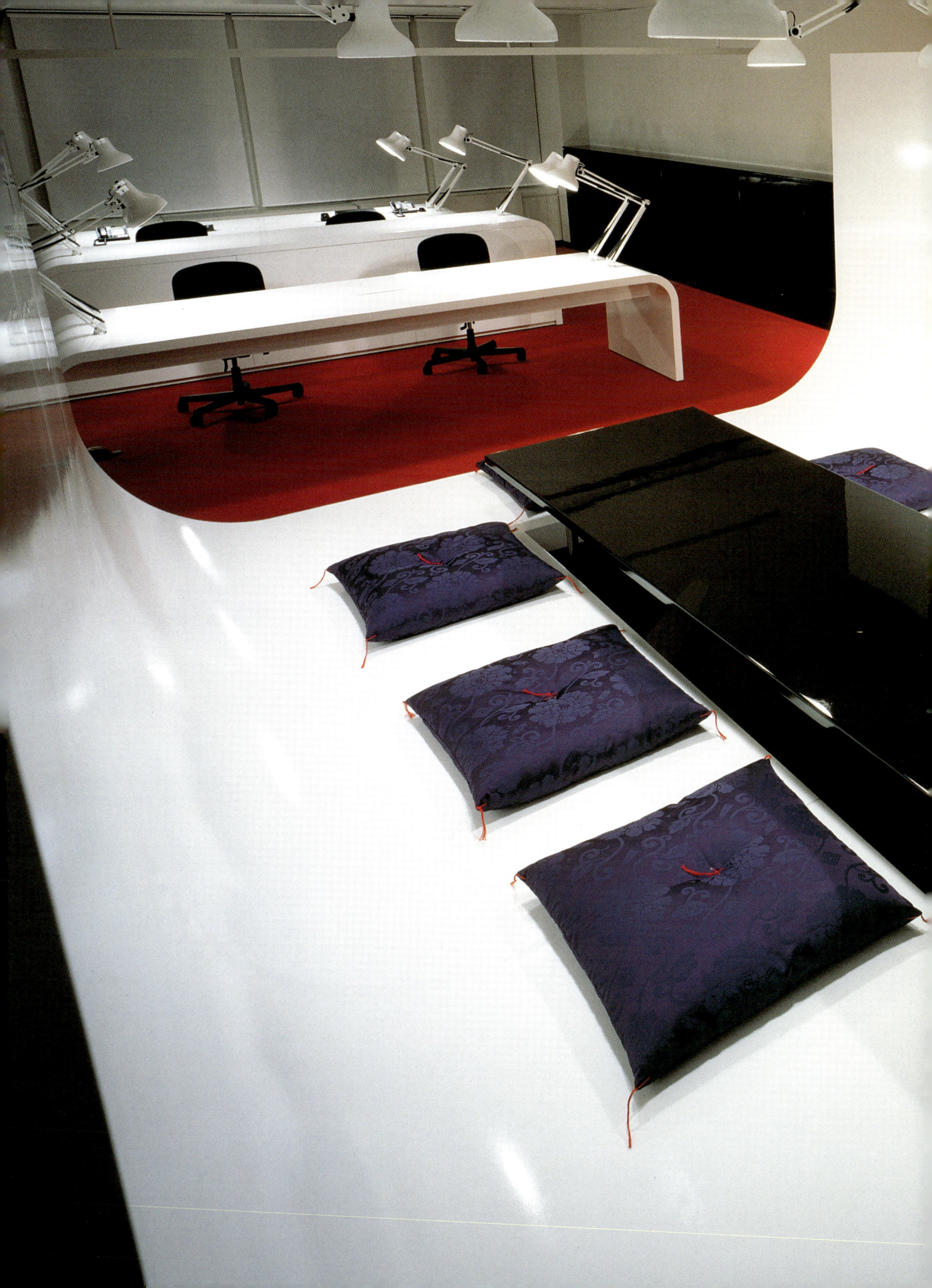

I am sure that their life in Japan over the last ten years or so has been accompanied by more difficulties than we can imagine. This is because our country is so matter-of-fact, boorish and unromantic, a marked contrast to Klein Dytham's characteristic sense of style and wit

Sense of Style

According to Toyo Ito, designs by Klein Dytham architecture neither melt invisibly into the background nor make an excessively expressionistic splash.

Mark Dytham and Astrid Klein are two of Japan's most individualistic designers. Perhaps the following is obvious because they are not Japanese, but their method of working, way of thinking and approach to architecture and furniture design is completely different from our own. This may not be completely apparent to those who simply look at their finished designs, but working with them makes it unmistakably clear. Although several foreigners have worked at my office from time to time, I have never felt as much difference between them and us as I have with these two – a difference that most likely can be ascribed to character.

Putting this difference into words is not as easy as it may seem, even though conventional terms such as 'sense', 'style' and 'wit' do come to mind. Using these words still leaves a certain and vital difference unexpressed and inexpressible, however. There is something deeper that cannot be qualified simply by stating that these architects have good design sense or that their sense of humour expresses a certain style.

Their personal sense of style comes from the way in which they live. Style is an essential part of their existence and a sense of humour their gift to society. This is demonstrated not only at a superficial level in their designs but also in every aspect of their daily life. Each interaction with others – speaking, wearing, eating, writing letters, giving presents – is a parallel to their design of architecture and furniture. The act of design, therefore, is neither more nor less important than their day-to-day activities. The level of design they have achieved springs from and supports their natural sensibilities. As a result, they find it unnecessary to stand on a soapbox and proclaim the meaning of, or the concept behind, their designs.

When I first met Astrid Klein and Mark Dytham twelve years ago, just after they had received their master's degrees, I was struck by their complete

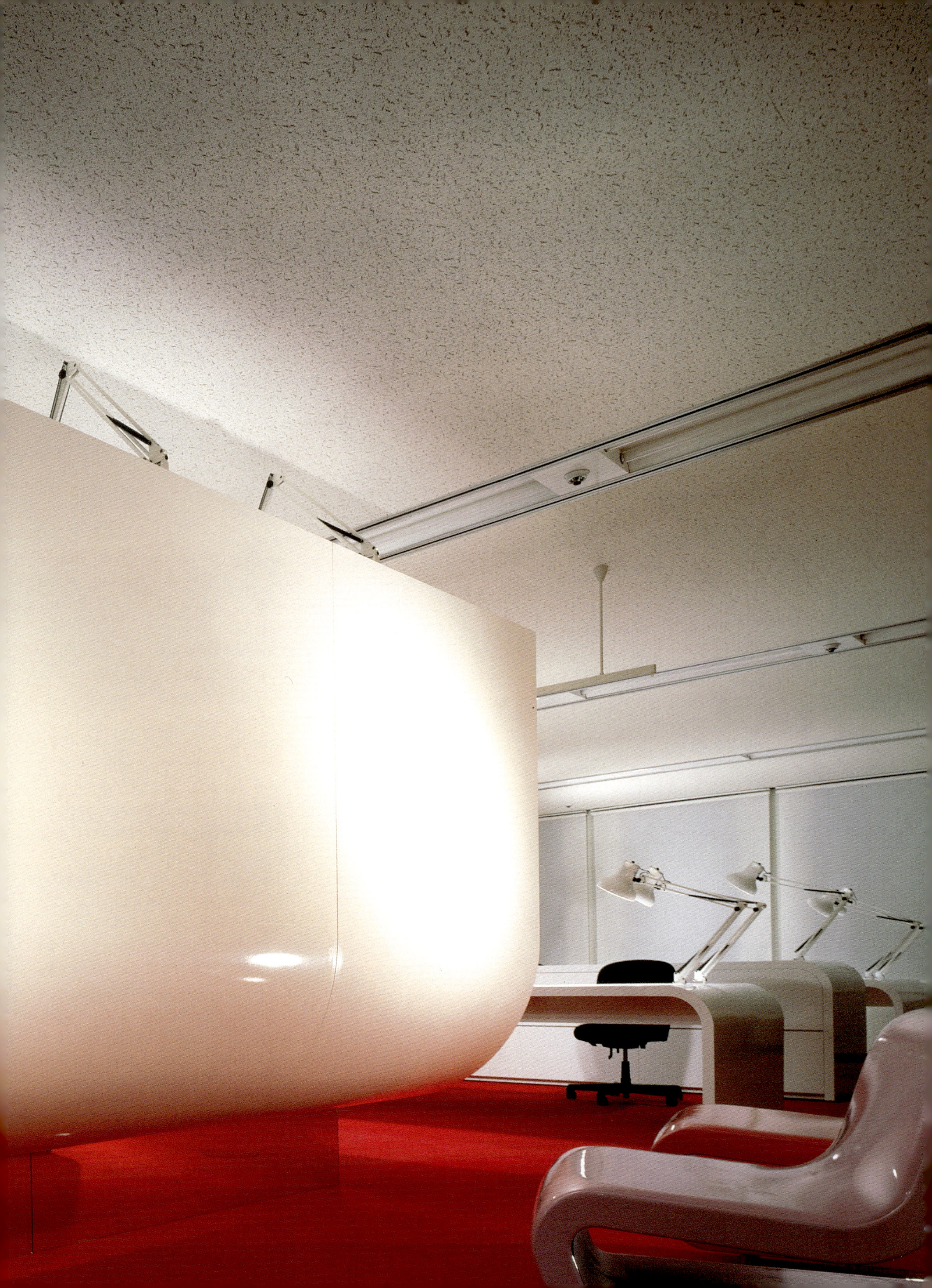

Bartle Bogle Hegarty
BARTLE BOGLE HEGARTY LTD.

Bartle Bogle Hegarty (2)

Location: Akasaka Twin Tower, Akasaka, Minato-ku, Tokyo / Client: Bartle Bogle Hegarty / General Contractor: D. Brain Co. Ltd / Start Design: March 1999 / Completion: September 1999 / Floor Area: 85 square metres / Furniture: Chu-Coo chair (Do-ing) / Wall: white UV-lacquer coated U-shape / Lighting: Z-lamp (Yamada Shomei) / Photography: Kozo Takayama

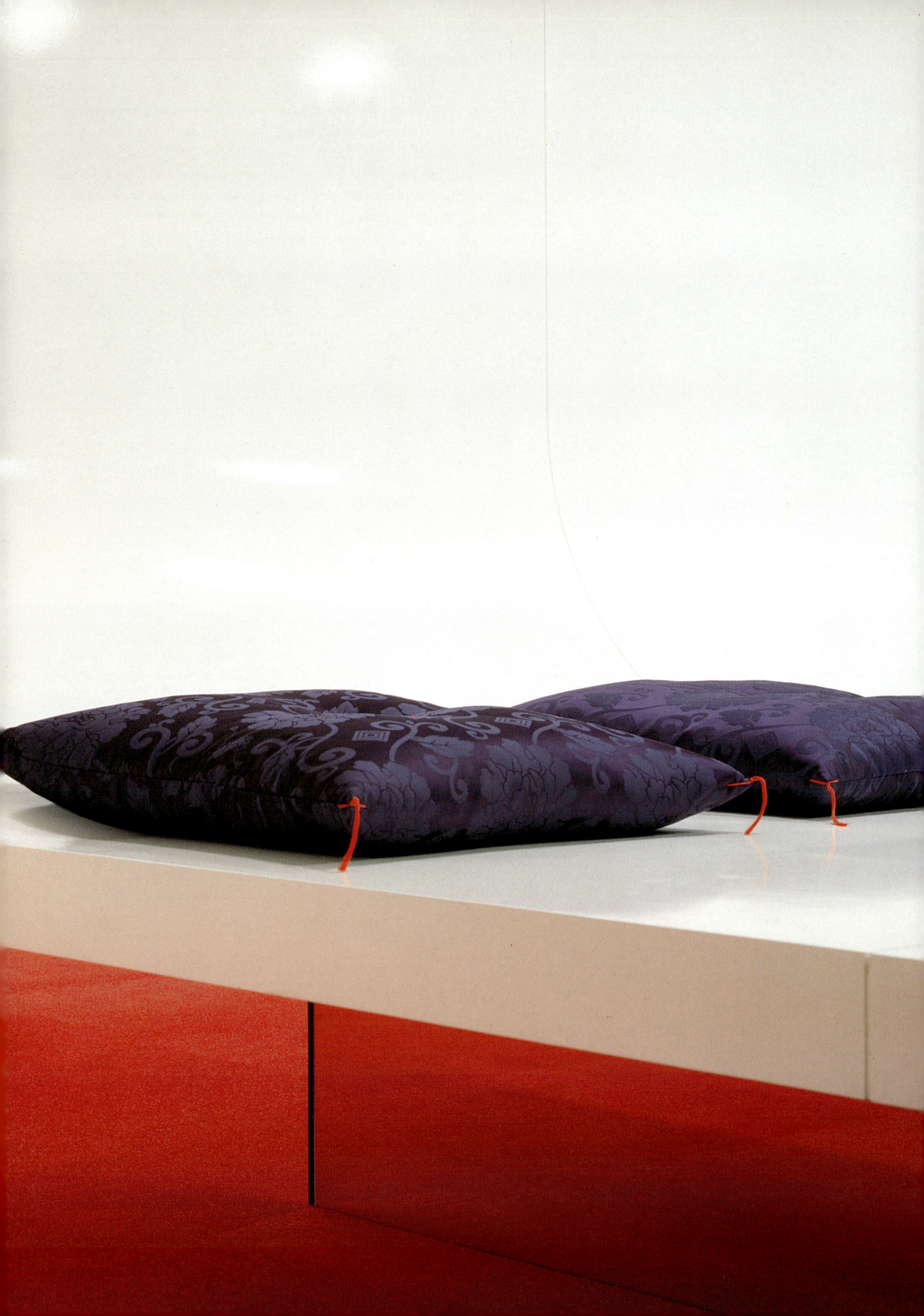

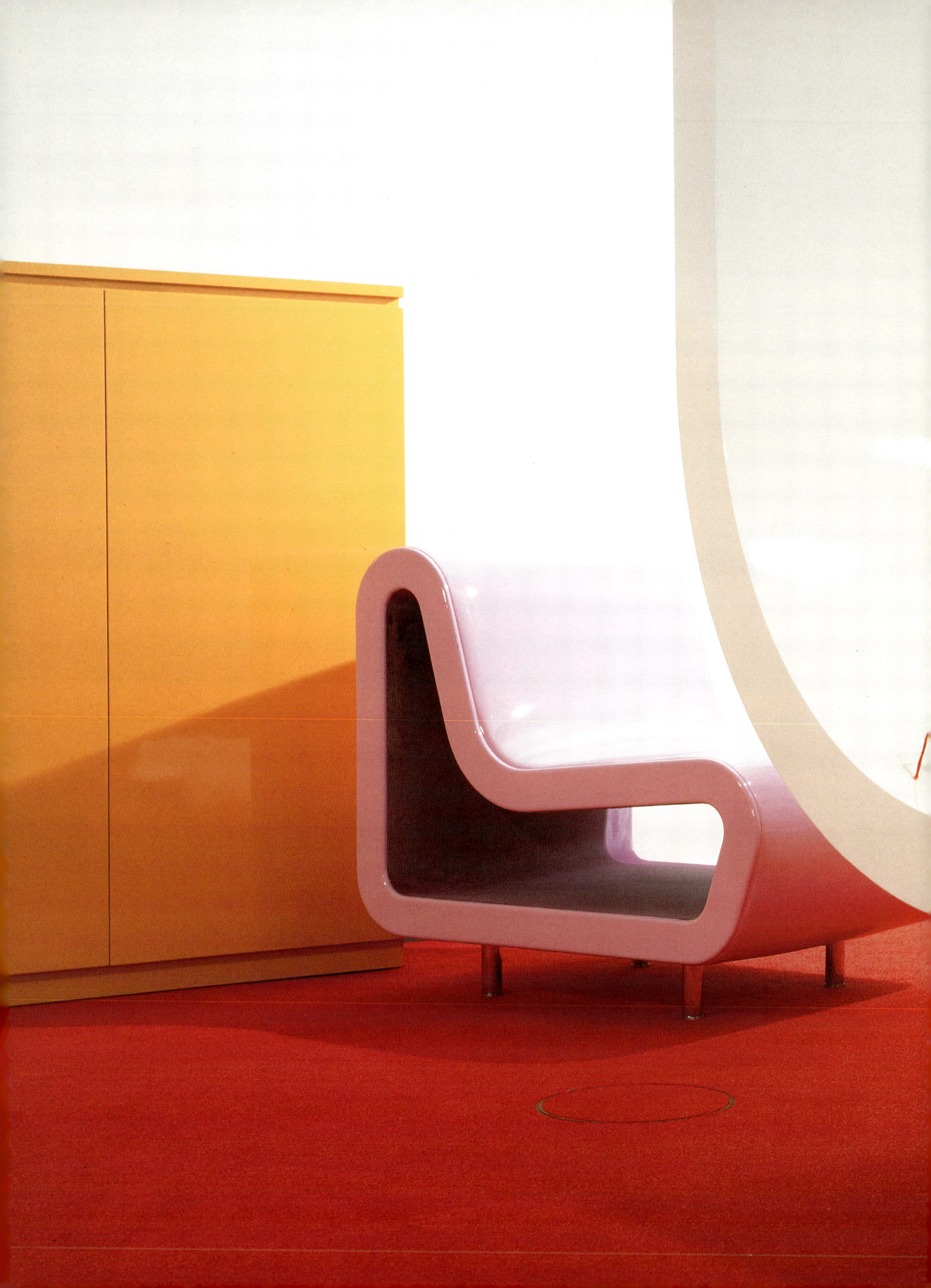

I do believe that design in Japan, both now and in the future, needs the kind of lively feeling, rooted in direct experience, that these two represent and utter sense of style. The absolute beauty of their presentation of the portfolio representing their years at the Royal College of Art — as they showed it to me, page by page — will forever remain in my mind. Their second visit to my office, upon their return from a trip to various parts of Japan, coincided with a request from a friend of mine for an interior-design project. I immediately decided to act as a go-between and to commission my young acquaintances to do this work, which became their first project in Japan: Sanae Ozeki Hair Salon in Ginza, central Tokyo.

Along with their professionalism, their rather austere design of mirrors on a large curving wall was evidence of a maturity and consideration of detail rarely found in first projects. The client was so pleased that he soon commissioned them for another job. Gradually their work began to find a place for itself in Japan.

I am sure that their life in Japan over the last ten years or so has been accompanied by more difficulties than we can imagine. This is because our country is so matter-of-fact, boorish and unromantic, a marked contrast to Klein Dytham's characteristic sense of style and wit. Although this attitude is changing in the younger generation, modern Japanese society in general possesses neither the sensibility nor the sensitivity needed for complete acceptance of such clever unconventionality. It seems as though this country lacks the fertile soil required to fully nourish their bright, light-hearted wit. Nothing is so tiring as communication without feedback.

Supporting Klein Dytham's designs is a sensitivity to the materials in which they work. Their projects and their use of building materials are always infused with discovery, whether it be balloons made from high-performance fabrics, experiments with polycarbonates, or sheets of MOW (a material made entirely of recycled plastic).

They neither attack nor praise current fashions. As exemplified by their use of balloons and MOW, KDa always looks for materials in the immediate vicinity when creating a design. They want interesting materials, but not something that melts invisibly into the background and not something

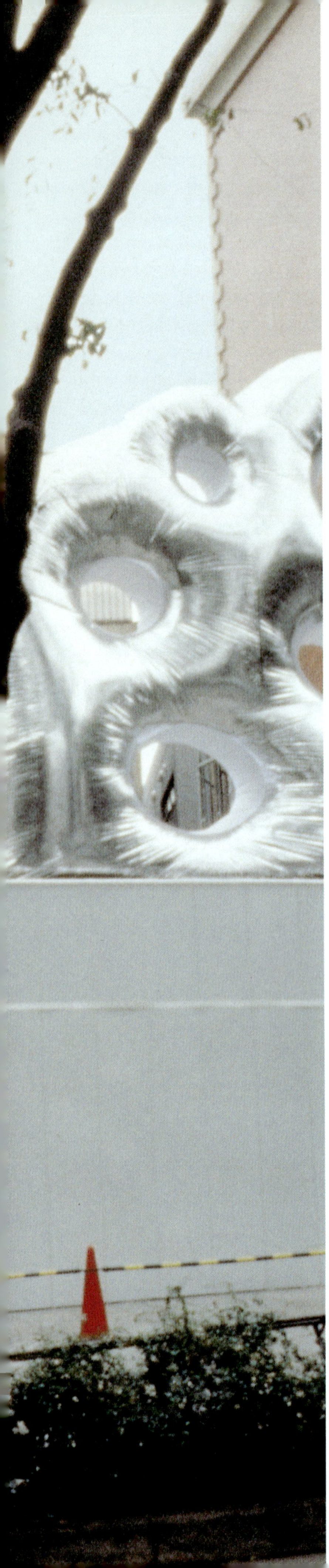
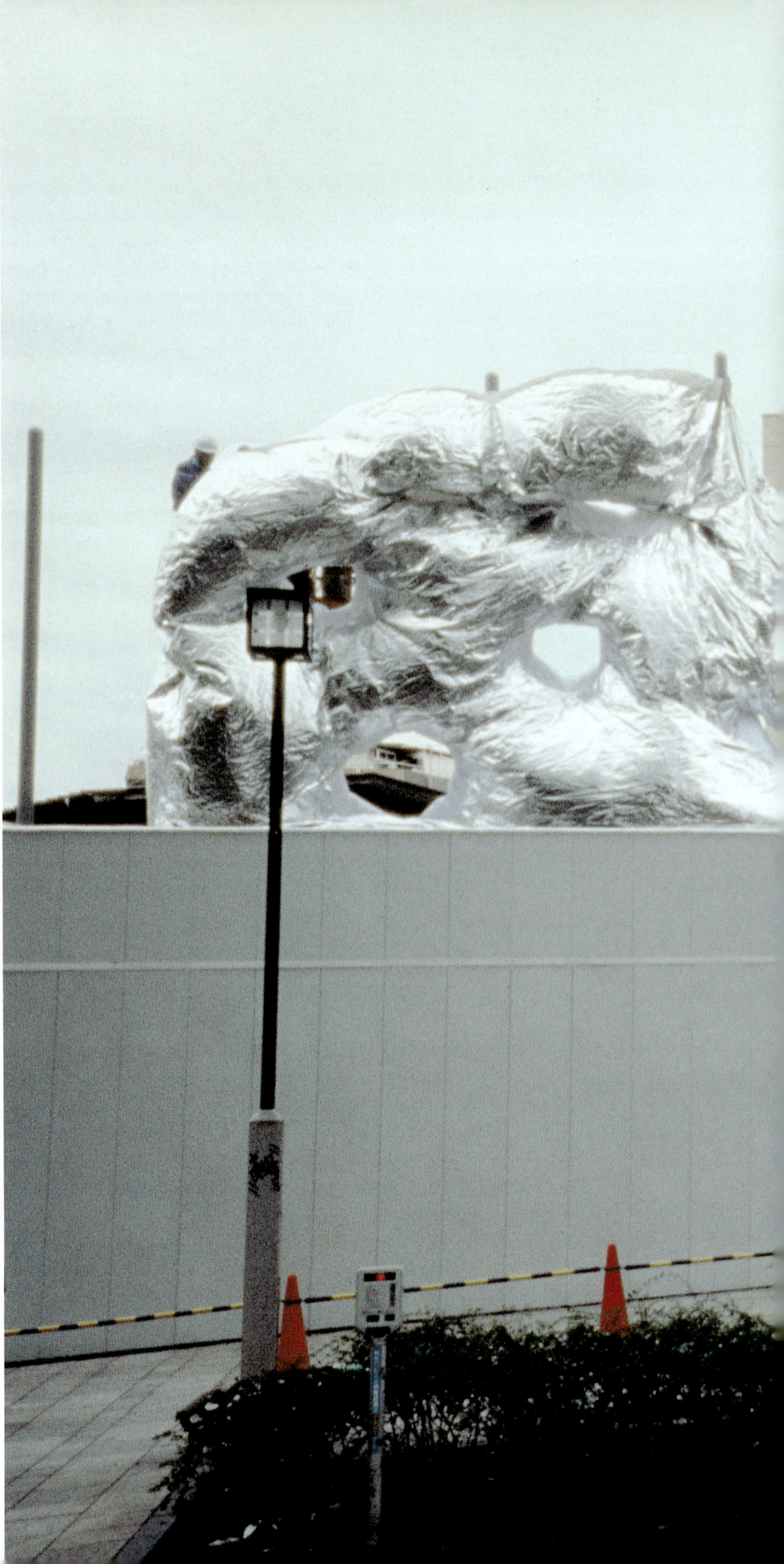

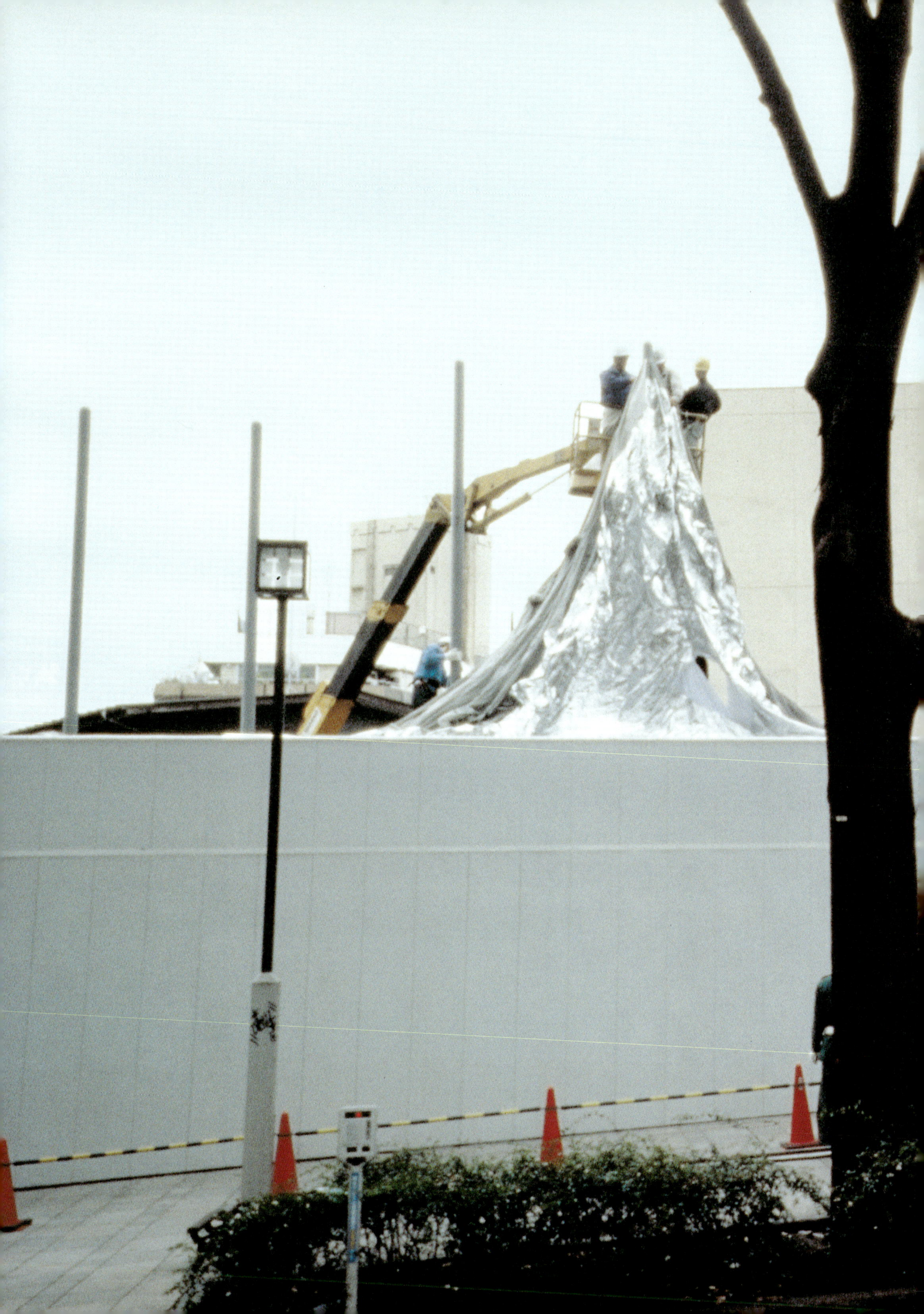

Pika-Pika Pretzel (1)

A hoarding to conceal construction work on a building site does not sound like a particularly exciting commission for an architect. International developer Veloqx asked KDa to create something eye-catching and distinctive to serve as a temporary structure enclosing a prominent site in Harajuku. As this was their first Tokyo development, Veloqx wanted to announce their arrival on the scene in Japan and also draw attention to the site. The project was split into two components, a hoarding while demolition work was in progress and one while the foundations were being laid. Intrigued by the irony of Japanese hoarding, usually covered with prints of flowers, woodland scenes or luscious ivy, KDa came up with their own interpretation of this tradition.

Splashed in huge letters across the structure during demolition was one single word – sumimasen: Japanese for 'sorry' – apologising for the noise, dust and trucks. As the client was also keen to let prospective tenants know how wide the building frontage was, KDa used the manga construction characters – usually portrayed bowing on most construction hoarding – holding a 34-metre-long tape.

After the building was demolished, phase two of the hoarding was inflated. Faced with a limited budget, and having worked with inflatables before, KDa knew that this was a sure way of achieving the maximum physical impact. The pretzels are made of the same high-tech fabric as high-altitude, round-the-world balloons. Large perforations form webs that connect the two sides of the inflatables together and help reduce wind loading. Made of translucent fabric, the sides of the holes glow after nightfall when the inflatables are illuminated from within. Pika pika is Japanese for shiny.

Location: Jingumae, Shibuya-ku, Tokyo / Client: Veloqx / Balloon Manufacturer: Cameron Balloons / Start Design: June 1999 / Hoarding Period: November 1999 - May 2000 / Size: 34 metres long, 10 metres high, 1 metre deep / Balloon: high-performance silver nylon fabric, inflated by fans / Photography: Katsuhisa Kida

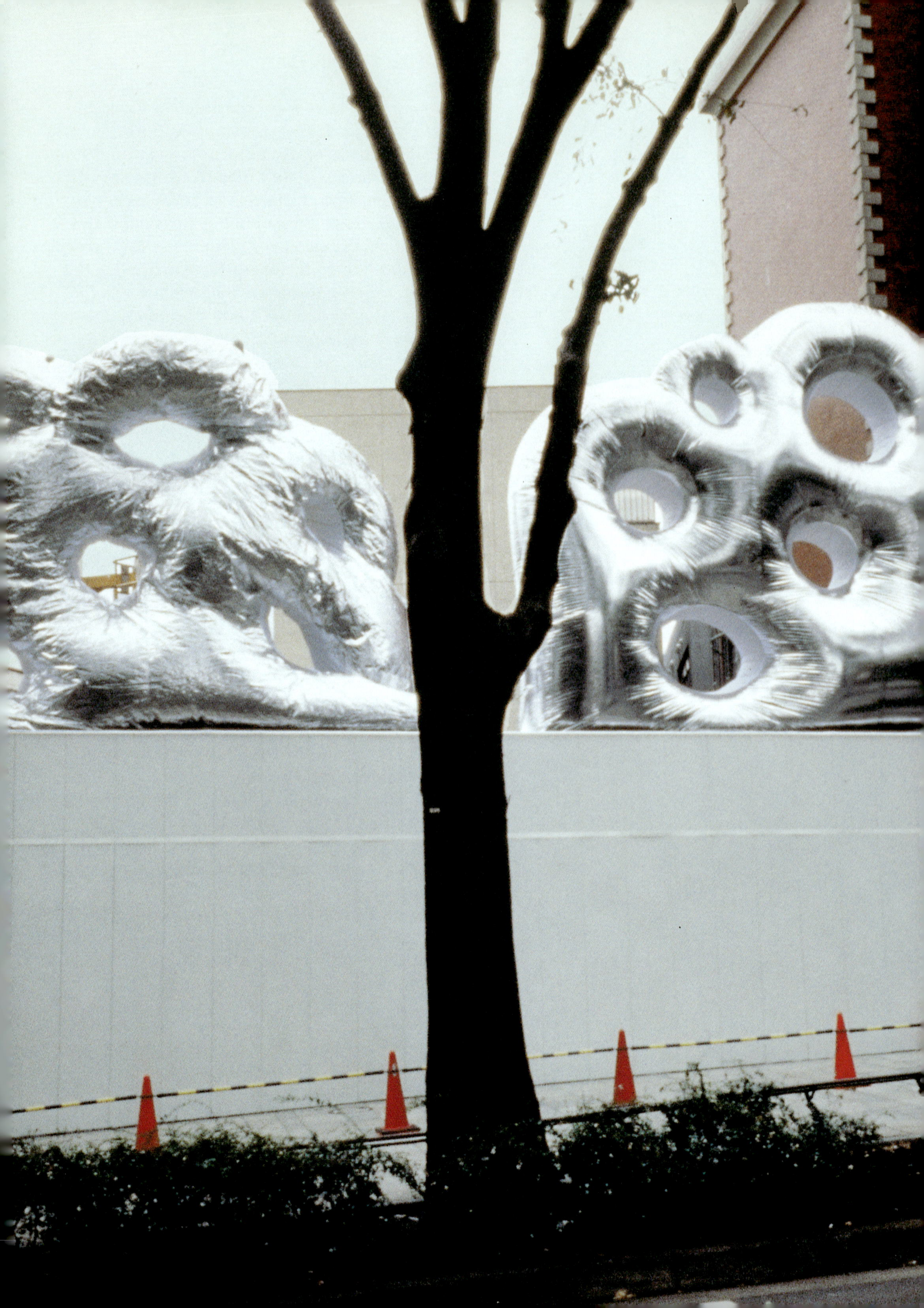

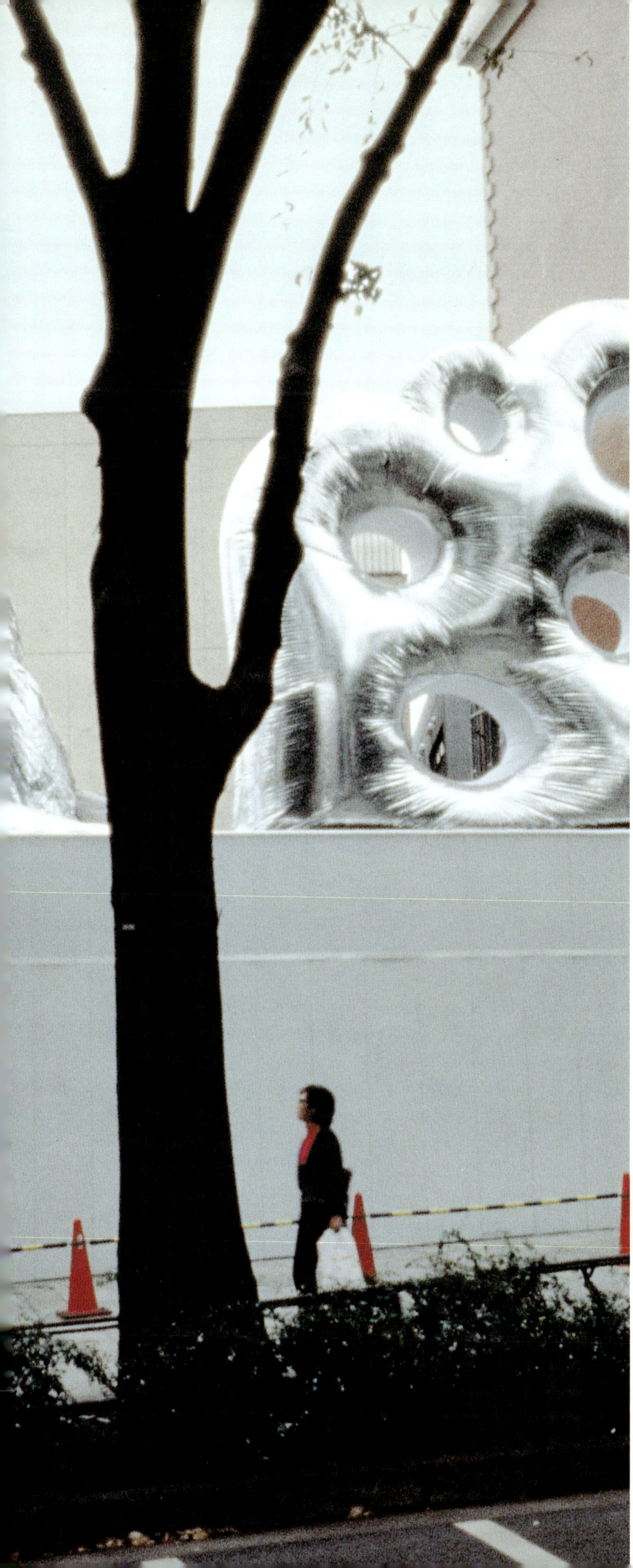
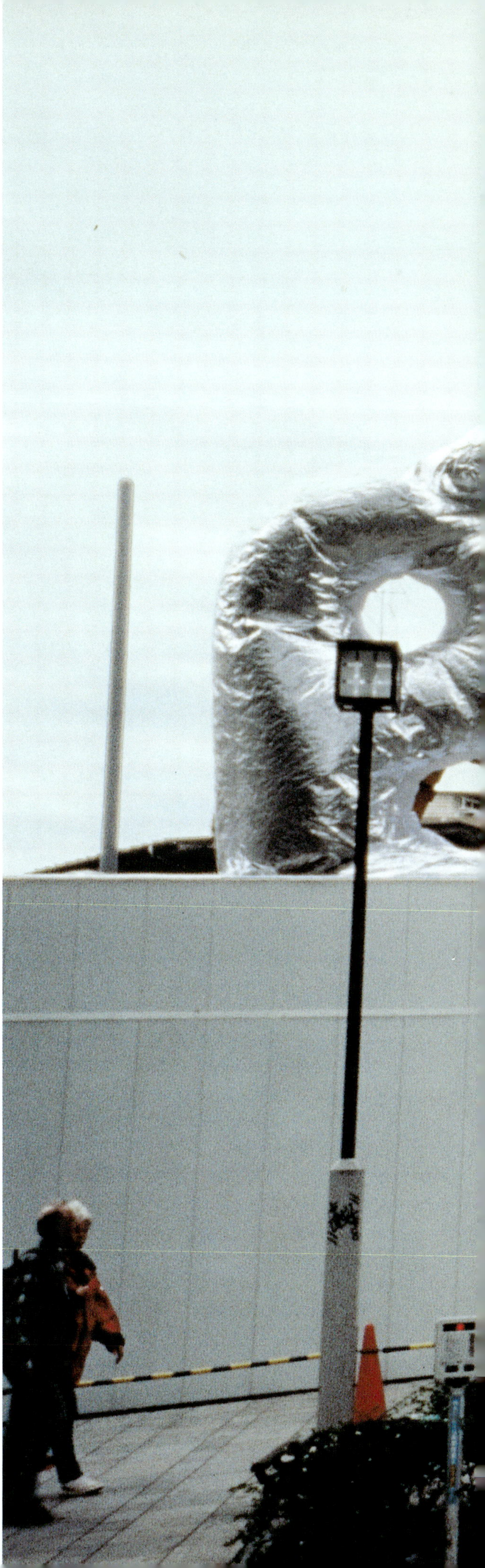

Mark Dytham and Astrid Klein are two of Japan's most individualistic designers that is excessively expressionistic. Materials, proportions and form – everything about their designs comes directly from their own physical reality. In other words, each project is proof that their language, in and of itself, is a natural expression of a refined, elegant physical reality.

I do believe that design in Japan, both now and in the future, needs the kind of lively feeling, rooted in direct experience, that these two represent. The type of society they propose is not one in which a sharply transparent or super-flat design freezes the user, but one in which we find an expression of maturity and friendliness. Klein and Dytham show us, time and again, what truly stylish design is.

Toyo Ito is a Japanese architect and the winner of numerous awards. His architecture practice, Toyo Ito & Associates, has been operating in Tokyo since 1971. Recent projects include an exhibition pavilion for Expo 2000 and the Sendai Mediatheque.

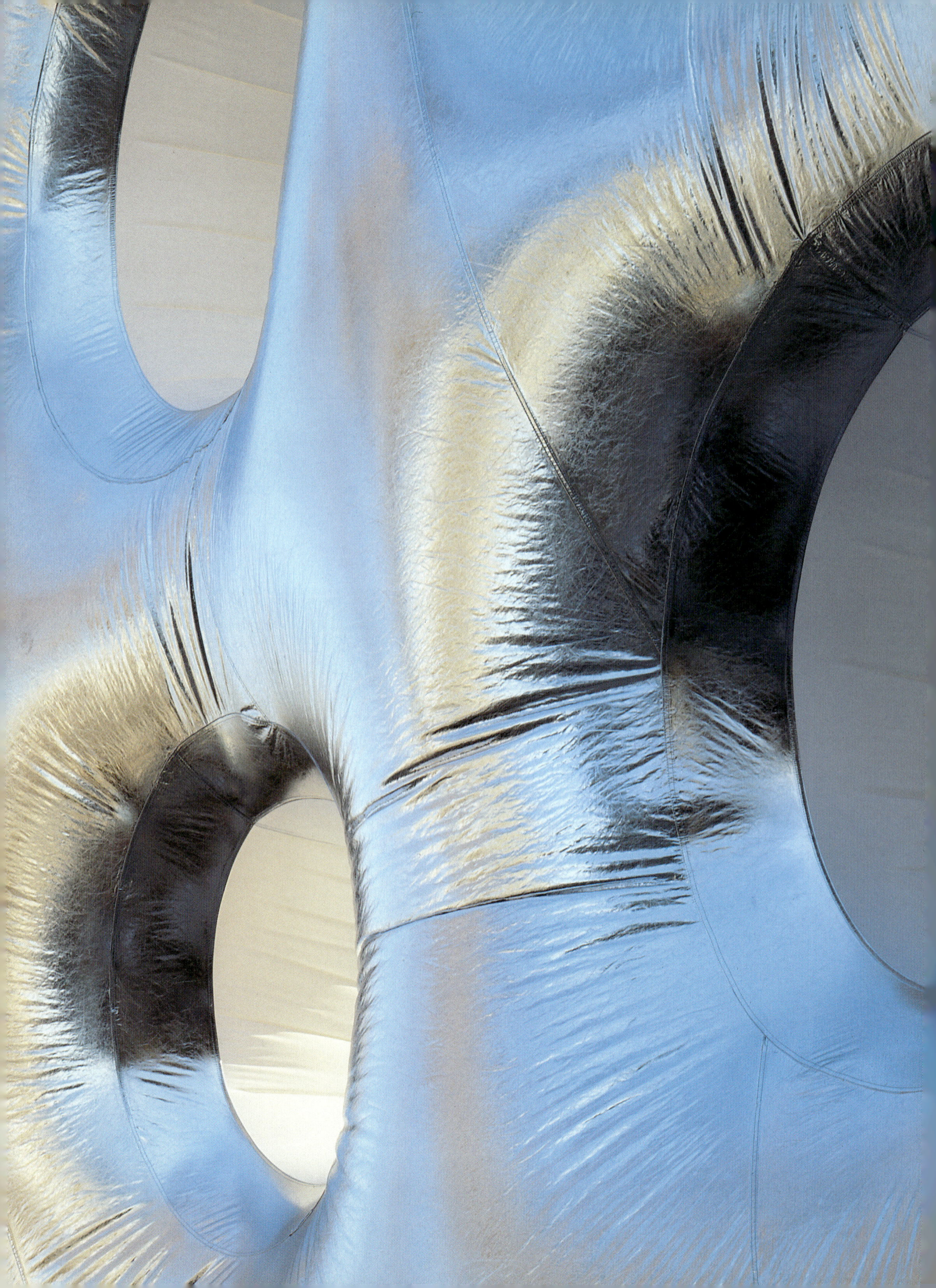

DELUXE!
BUBBLE DESIGN
KLEIN DYTHAM
ARCHITECTURE
HAPPY
HARAJUKU'S
BRIGHTEST
SPOT
参上!
EXPOSURE!

Pika-Pika Pretzel (2)

神宮前
神宮前出張所
Jingumae Branch Office
神宮前区民会館
Jingumae Community Hall
心身障害者福祉センター
Welfare Center for the Disabled
国民銀行

HAPPY

34m WIDE

HARAJUKU'S BRIGHTEST ピカピカ SPOT

FREE EXPRESSION

Klein Dytham's skill in gathering together an impressively varied assortment of people is nothing if not indicative of their overwhelming presence

Creating a Scene

Chiharu Watabe thanks Klein Dytham architecture for its exciting contribution to a gradually developing Tokyo design scene.

Whether at home in Japan or abroad, I'm always surprised by the proliferation of interior-design magazines in bookstores specialising in art, a phenomenon that has emerged within only the past five years. Interior-design magazines have also become regulars in the fashion and culture sections of ordinary bookshops and on a great many magazine racks. The trend is particularly predominant in Europe, where designers experimenting in the areas of fashion and culture base their ideas on both a sense of purpose and a focus on individuality. A strong enough combination of purpose and individuality, along with designers who aren't afraid to step over the line, can raise a creative discipline – be it music, fashion or interior design – to a level that we refer to as a 'scene'.

A good example is London. Several British designers organise their own exhibitions, give parties and sponsor other promotional events. Such activities encourage interaction among those in product and interior design, fashion and music. This exciting mix ultimately evolved into the London design scene. For the UK98 exhibition English designer Ben Kelly came up with True Stories while being fully involved with the overall direction of the project. Colleague JAM sells its work directly to businesses and simultaneously plays the role of design consultant.

Back home in Japan, Tokyo Designer's Week and Happening – events that resemble 100% Design and Designers Block London – have merged in recent years with a bigger stage for independent designers and more shelf space for interior-design magazines to produce a watered-down version of the European-style design scene. Many such events in Japan, however, come across as one-off exhibitions organised solely for designers. Their resemblance to similar shows and trade fairs in London and Milan is just that: similar.

No one is working harder to energise the Tokyo design scene than Klein Dytham architecture.

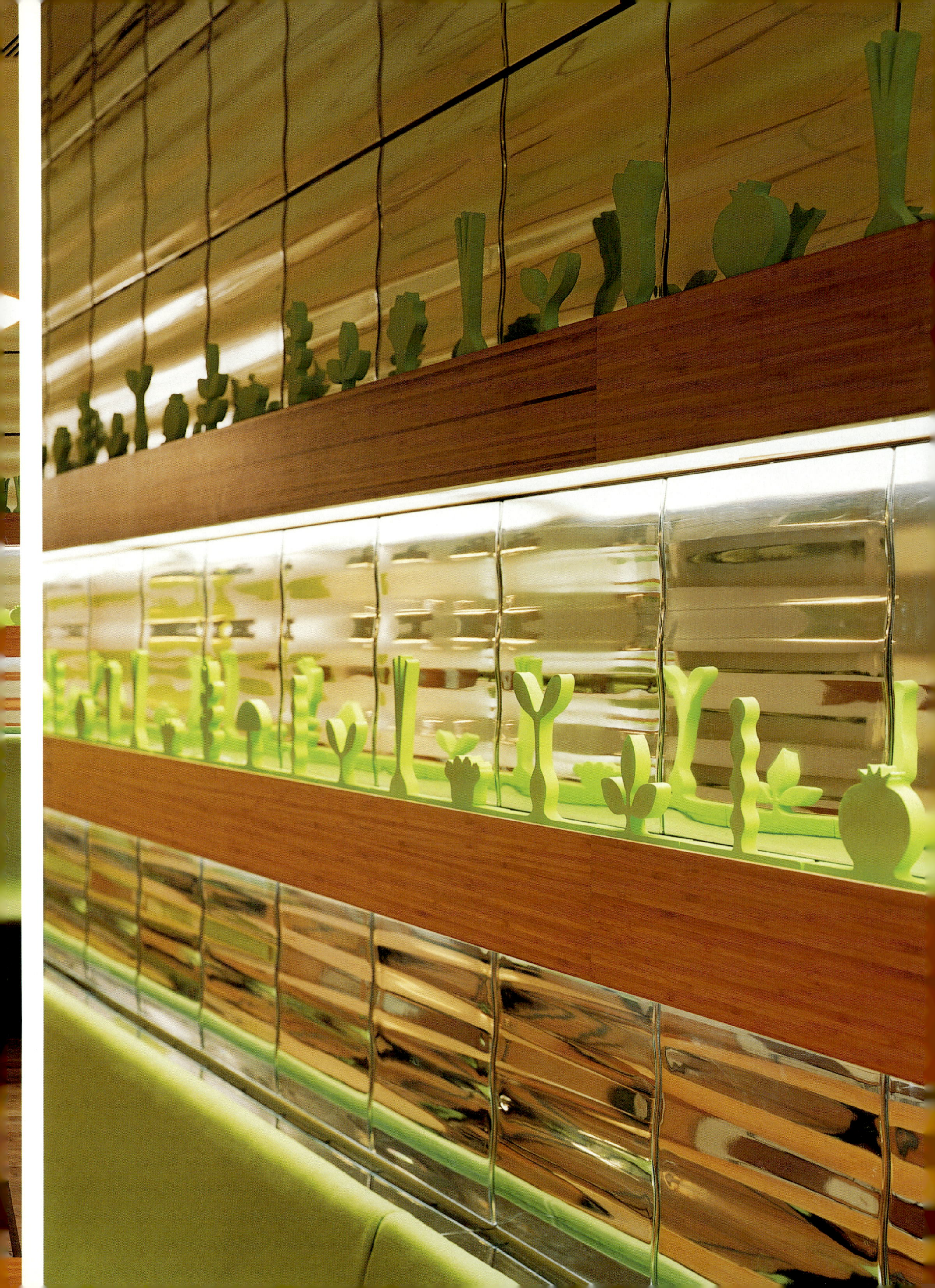

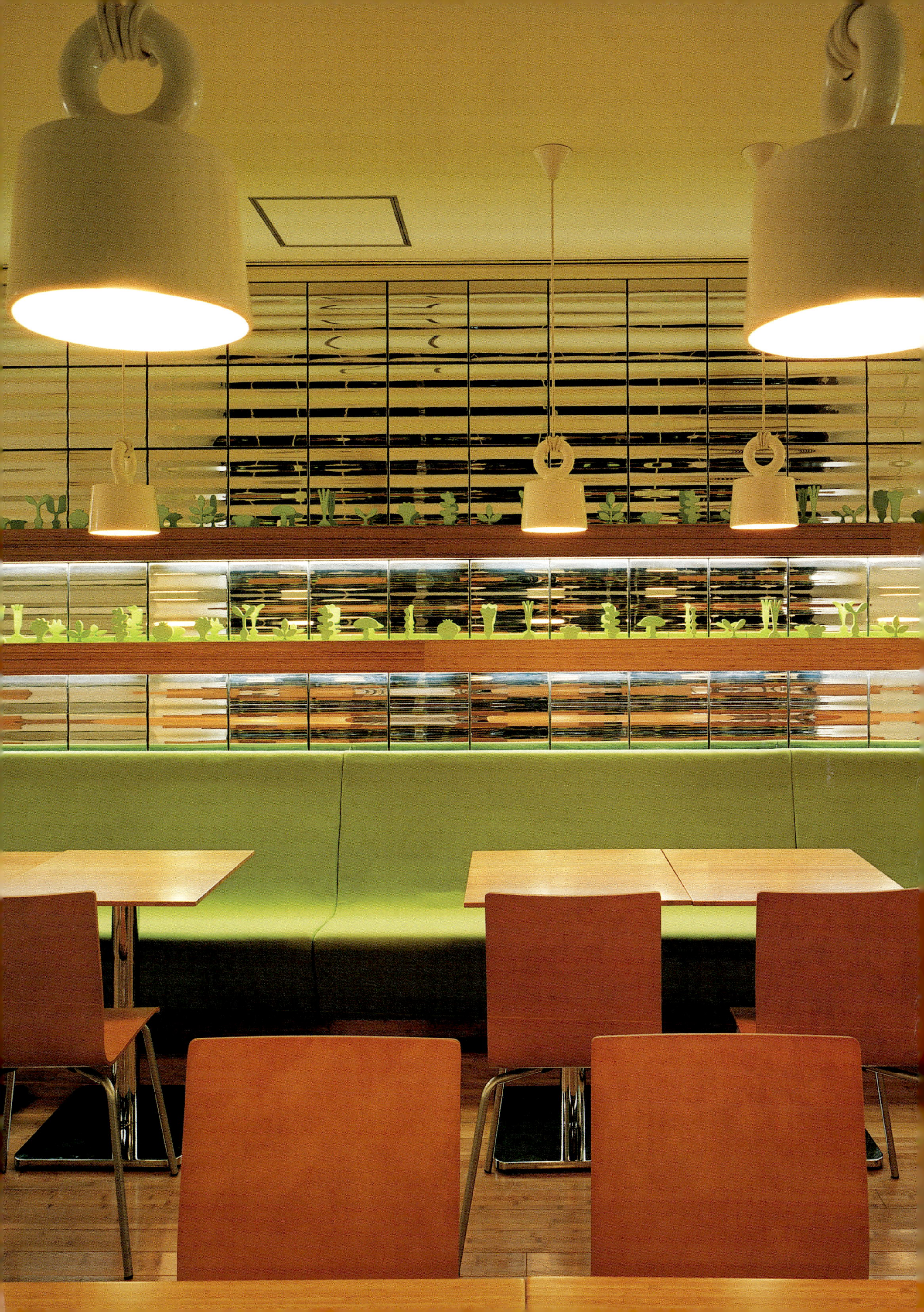

Vegie-To-Go

Vegie-To-Go is a café-deli serving healthy meals for the young and trendy crowd of Daikanyama. Bright green spongy pictograms of vegetables form the eye-catching features in the simple elongated space. Orders for eat-in or take-away meals are taken at the entrance counter, and further inside is seating for forty people. Entirely clad in wavy mirror panels, the rear wall reflects daylight entering through the window to the street and distorts the reflections of the rows of spongy vegetables loosely pasted onto shelves in front.

It remains to be seen just how long their vivid green colour freshens up the space dominated by the natural sliced bamboo of the floor and furnishings.

Location: Daikanyama-cho, Shibuya-ku, Tokyo / Client: Best Bridal Co. Ltd / Logo Design: Namaiki / General Contractor: D. Brain Co. Ltd / Start Design: January 2000 / Open: August 2000 / Floor Area: 46 square metres, 38 seats / Lighting: molle shae ceiling lamp (Idée) / Floor: bamboo flooring (Idée) / Wall: wavy mirror panel (IKEA), green polyurethane cookie cutter shoots (Toast) / Photography: Kozo Takayama

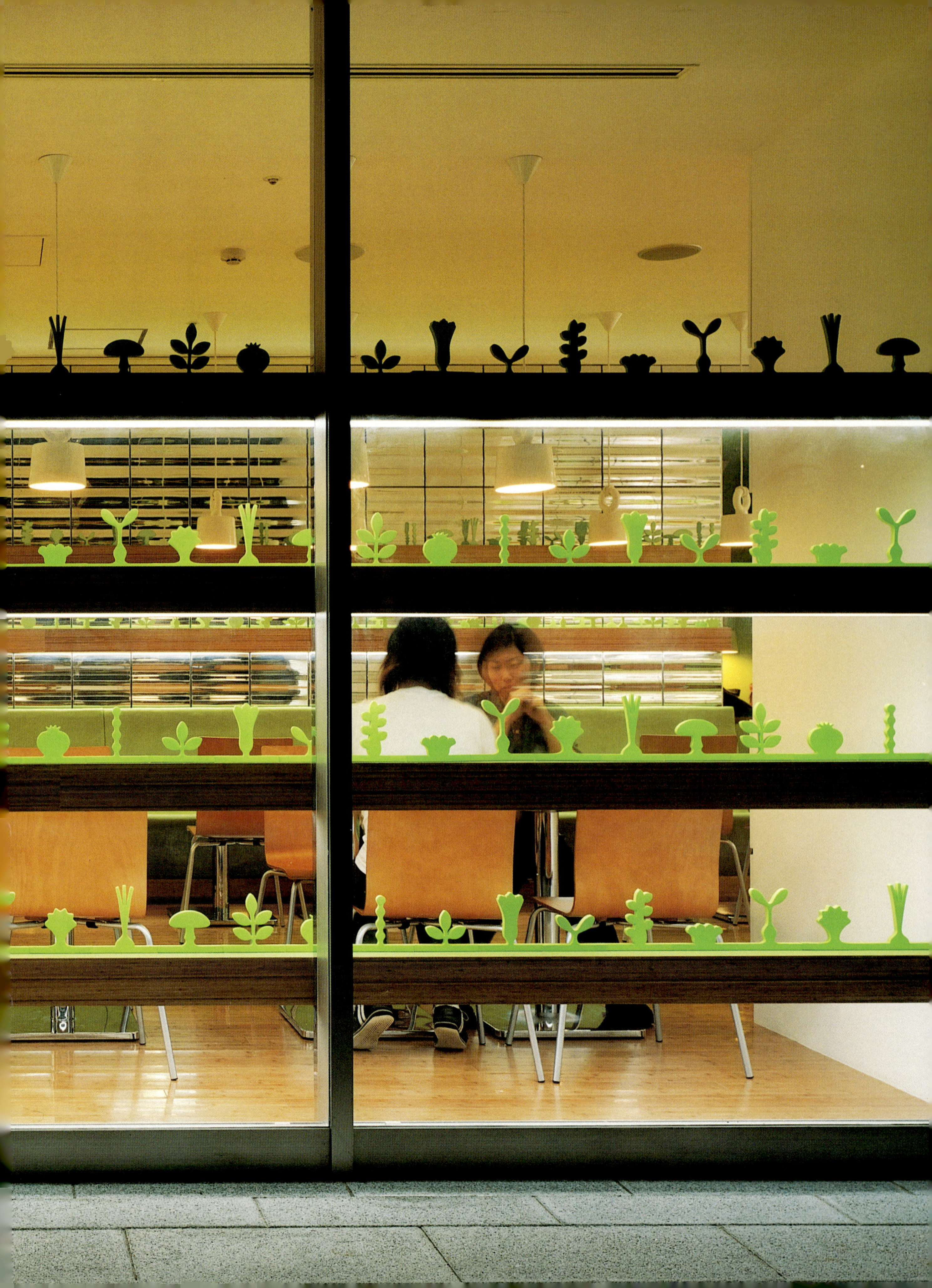

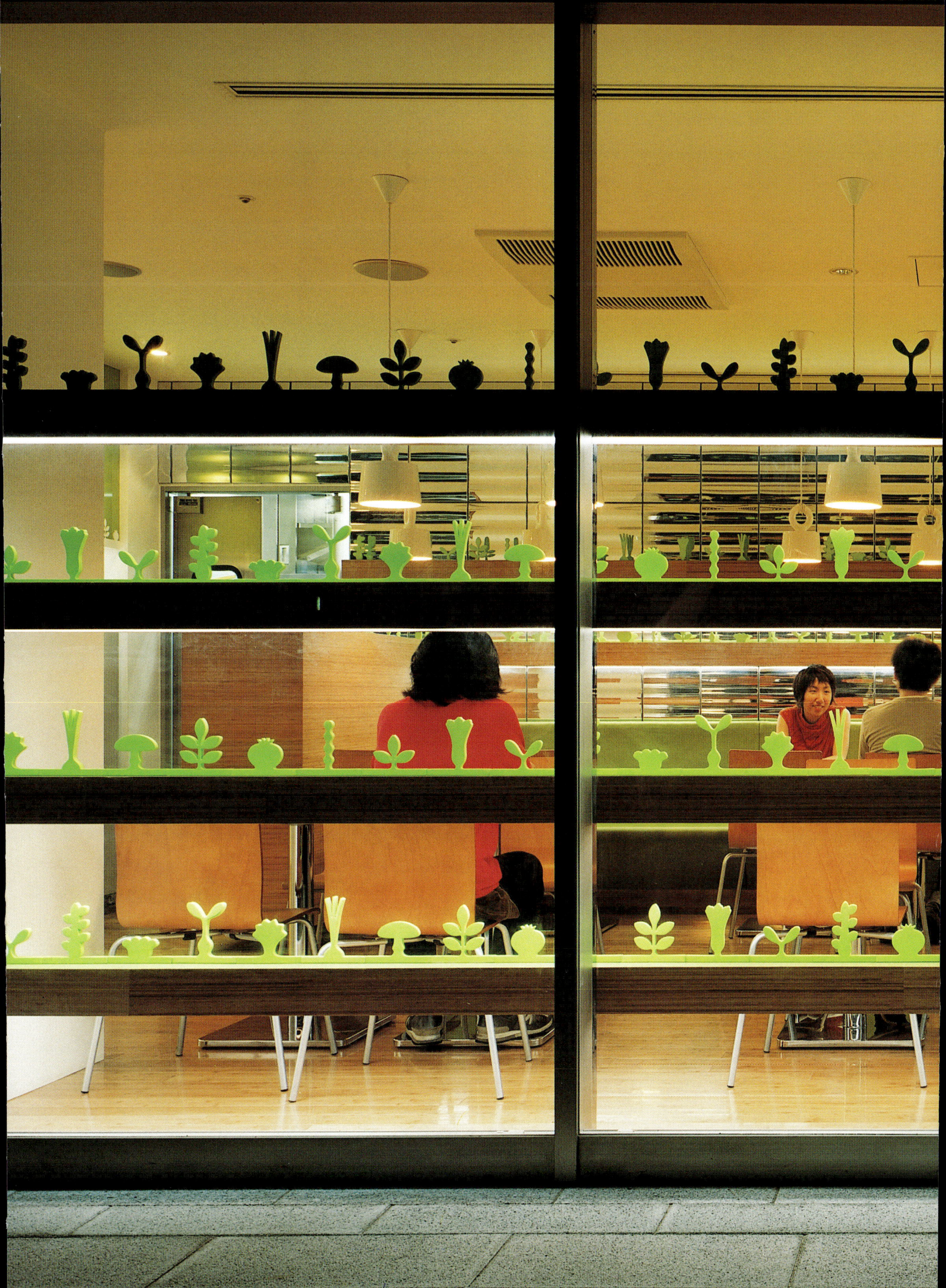

In giving free rein to their curiosity, KDa created an amazingly popular site that receives over 10,000 page hits a day from a wide variety of surfers

Although architects at heart, Astrid Klein and Mark Dytham are also active in the areas of interior and product design. Their gift lies in an ability to see each project from a number of different angles and to enjoy and develop what they discover, even if it has little or nothing to do with the original concept.

The interior that Klein Dytham designed in 2000 for Bartle Bogle Hegarty, an international advertising agency, revolves around a centrally positioned meeting room that simulates the look of an inline-skating halfpipe. When the same conference room appeared in the December '99 issue of Esquire, however, the space was described as a private bedroom in an airport lounge!

Chu-Coo, a collection of furniture that Klein Dytham designed for NHK Nagano Broadcast Centre, is available for purchase from the architects' website (www.klein-dytham.com). Selling products on line and thus bypassing shops and other standard distribution networks reflects the logical evolution of a contemporary outfit. The website itself is stunning. It not only functions as a portfolio of KDa's work but also introduces their favourite Japanese products (click on 'Fetish'), celebrity-studded ad campaigns ('Sold Out') and drink-can designs ('Canned'). In giving free rein to their curiosity, they've created an amazingly popular site that receives over 10,000 page hits a week from a wide variety of surfers.

A discussion of the firm's broad range of activities would be incomplete without a description of its office space, modestly dubbed Deluxe. Although the location in Azabu-Juban was hard to reach by public transport prior to the recent installation of a new underground line, I have visited KDa several times since the partners set up shop in 1998. The temptation to return to a place where something is always happening outweighs the inconvenience of getting there without a car. In addition to Klein Dytham, Deluxe is home to graphic, interior and sound designers, as well as a brewery.

The individual activities of these enterprises have spawned a number of collaborative efforts. Klein Dytham has worked with other Deluxe members on several projects. For example, Namaiki's graphics were part of KDa's design for

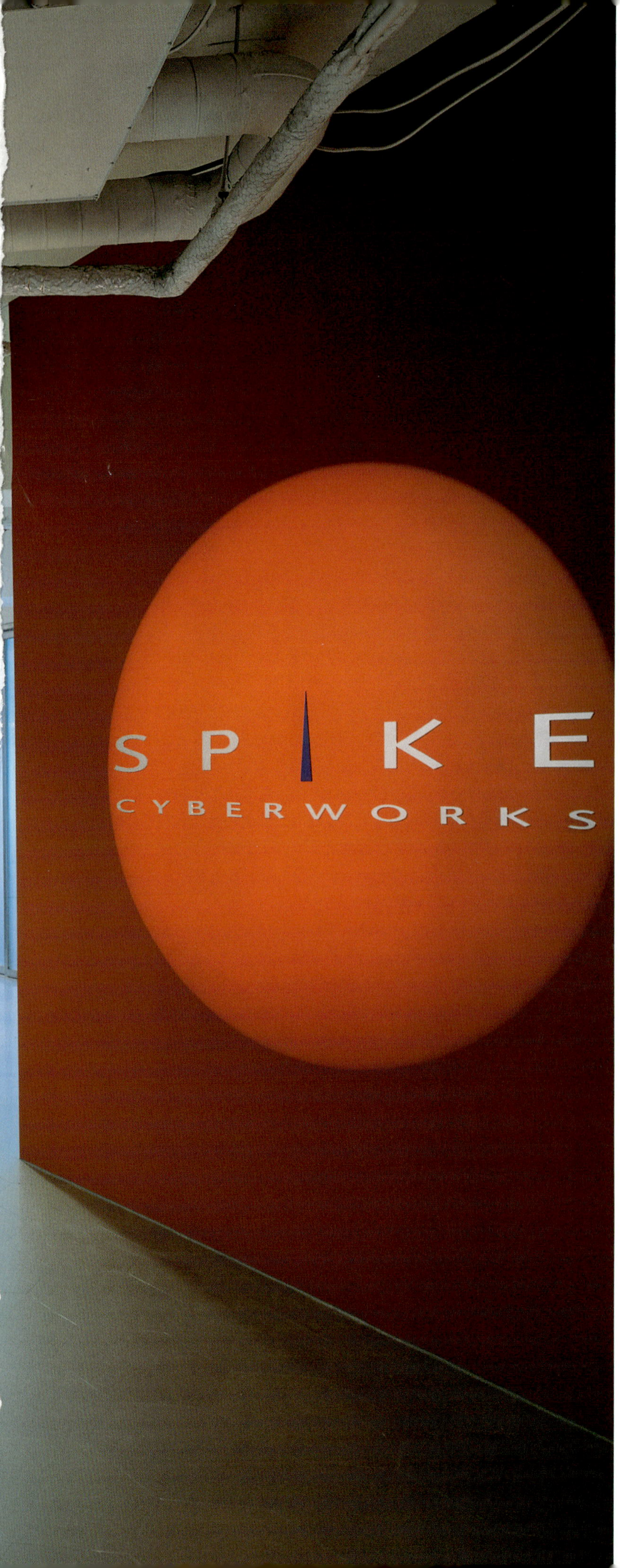
SPIKE
CYBERWORKS

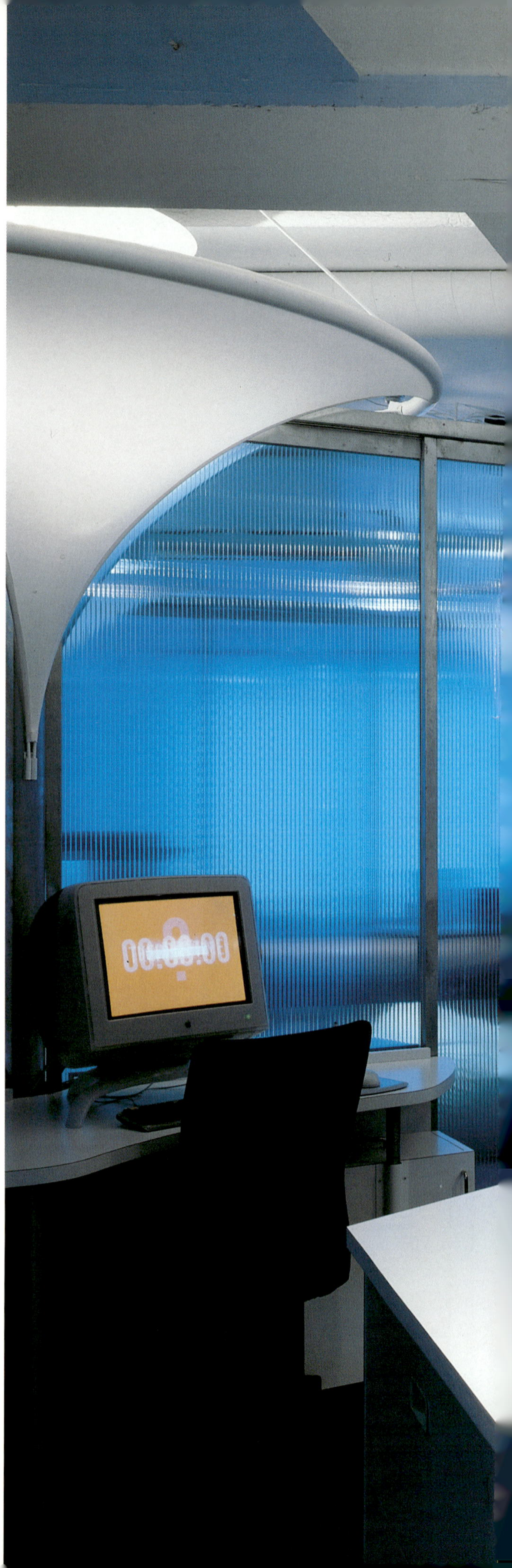

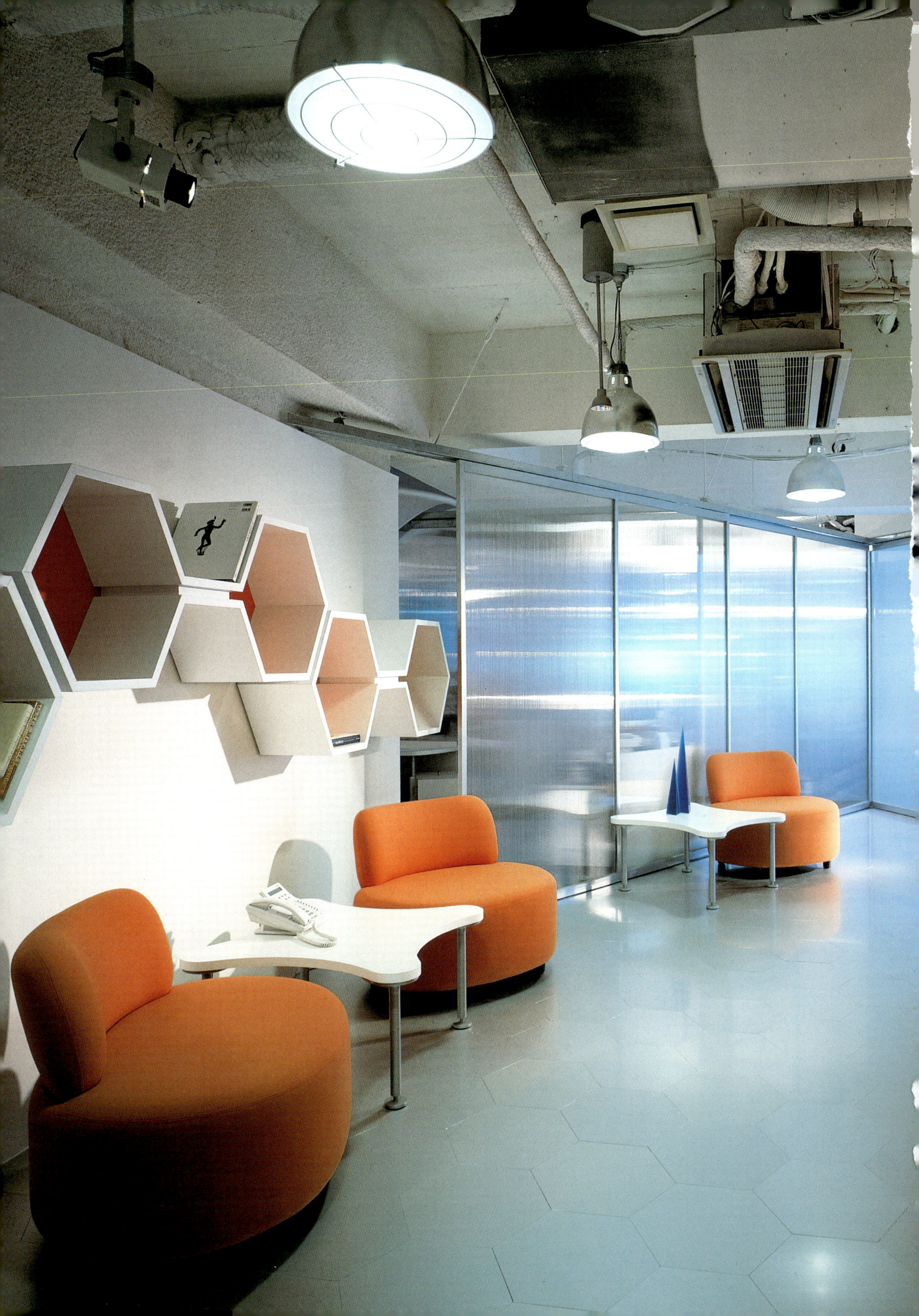

Spike Cyberworks

In web design the screen is the prime object on everybody's desk. Housed in a standard office building, Spike Cyberworks wanted a fresh, light and flexible environment to reflect the horizontal organisation of a web-based company.

In this project KDa chose a hexagonal shape for the centre of the office. At each corner of the honeycomb is a cluster of three desks. Located in the middle, a large hexagonal-shaped table further emphasises the office layout.

Separating the clusters are twin-wall polycarbonate screens finished in different hues of transparent blue film. When closed, the sliding screens define a more intimate hexagonal space; when open, everyone still has their own personal corner of space, though they share the larger space. To avoid glare on the screens, illumination is diffused by means of fan-shaped white covers stretched above each desk.

The blue screens give an intimate atmosphere to the space and create less brightly illuminated work areas further from the windows. The entrance area picks up on the honeycomb theme with hexagonal, mat aluminium floor tiles and bookshelves. The orange colour lightens up the entrance area and forms a fitting contrast to the blue colour of Spike's logo. The arrangement of sliding screens can totally separate the working area from the entrance and guide guests directly to the presentation rooms.

Location: Nihonbashi-muromachi, Chuo-ku, Tokyo / Client: Spike Cyberworks Japan Limited / General Contractor: D. Brain Co. Ltd / Start Design: May 2000 / Open: October 2000 / Floor Area: 248 square metres / Seating: OXO chairs (Hitch Mylius) for entrance, T-chair and TomVac (Vitra) for working area, Memo (Ron Arad and Inflate) for working area / Floor: hexagonal aluminium tiles for entrance / Sliding Doors/Glass: honeycomb core glass (Figla), twin-wall polycarbonate screens (Asahi glass) / Photography: Kozo Takayama

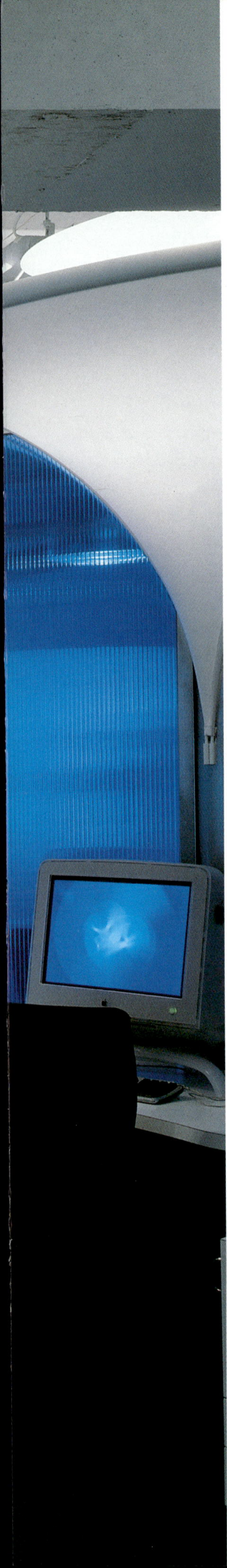
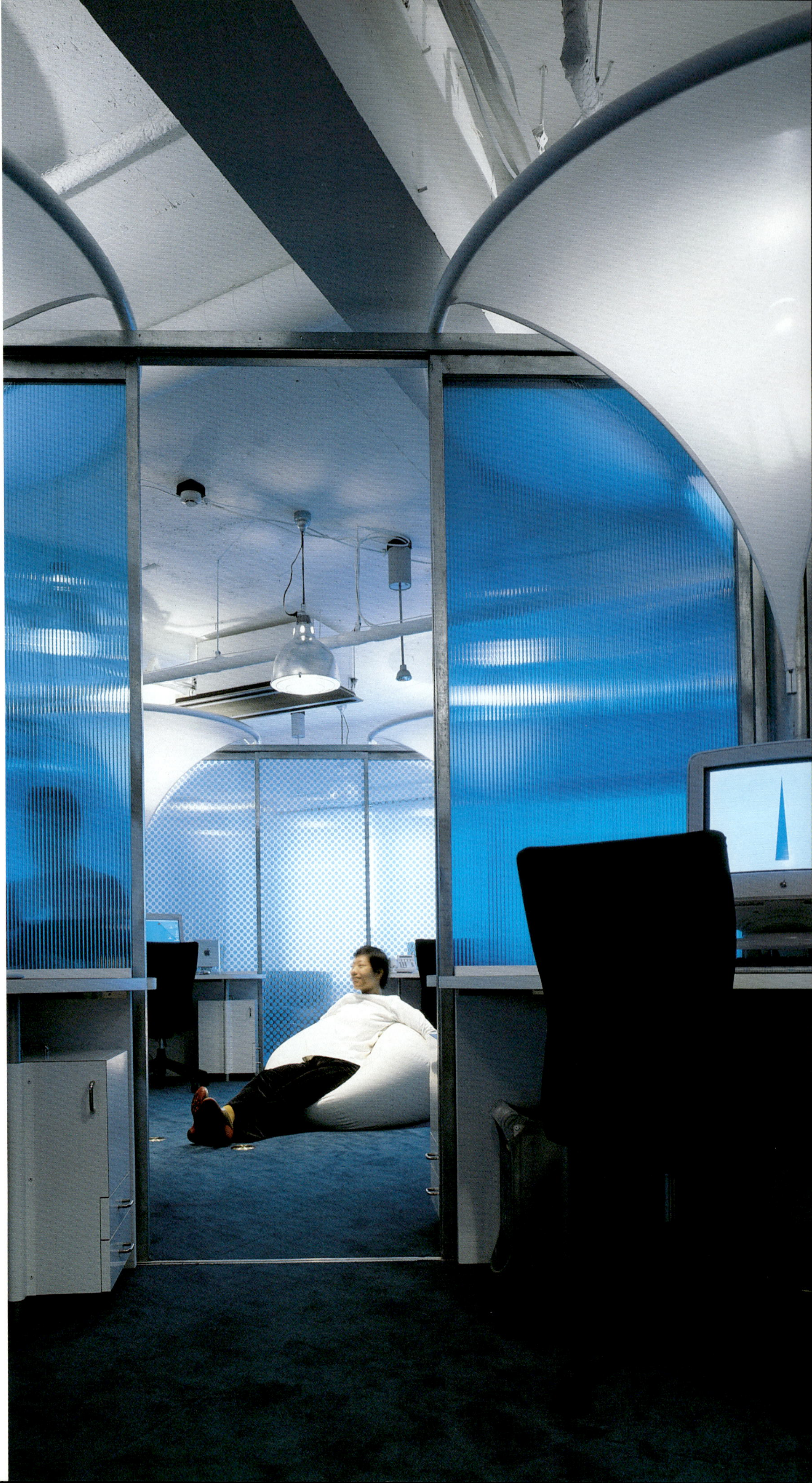

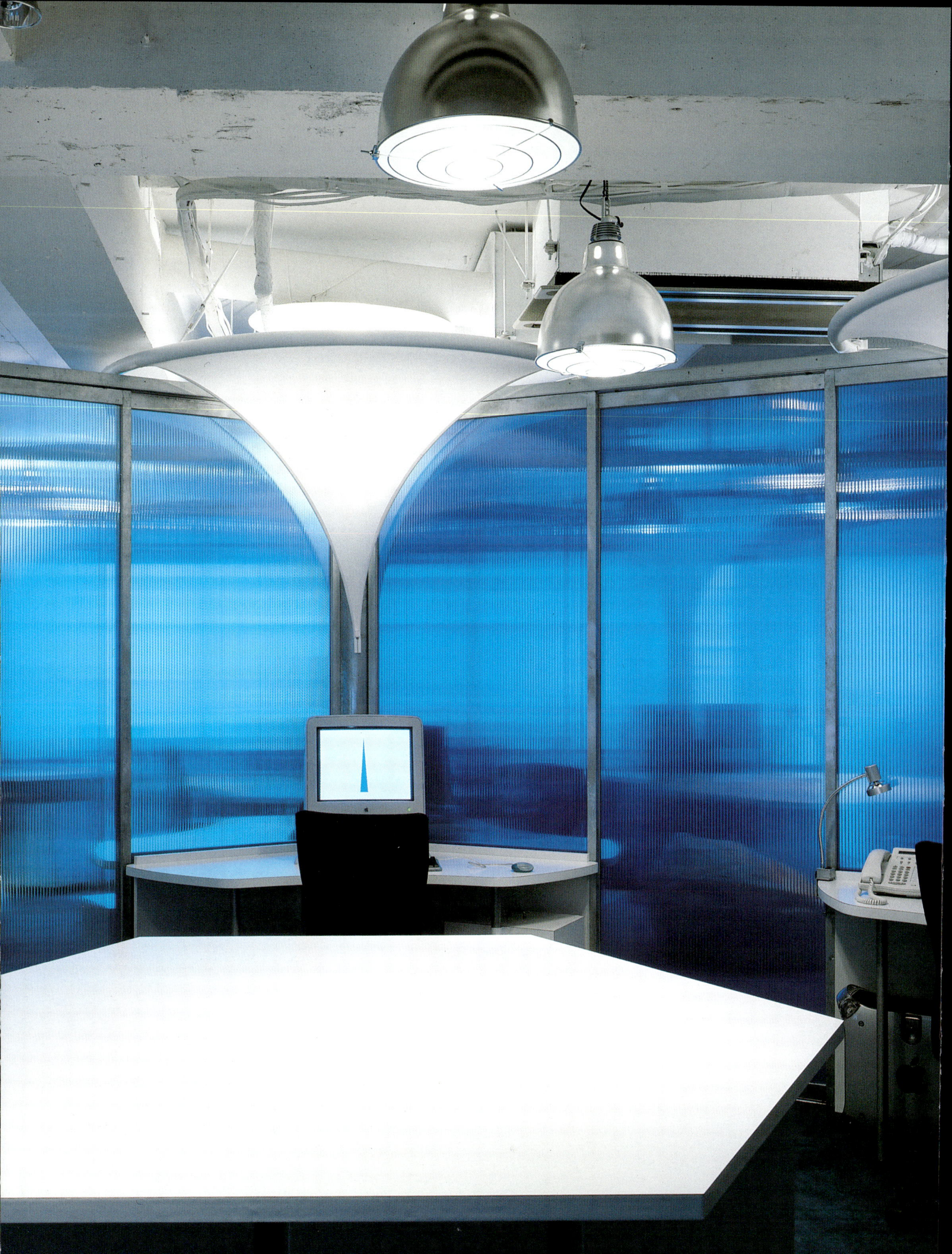

No one is working harder to energise the Tokyo
design scene than Klein Dytham architecture

the British Council Library, which won the Japan Library Association Architectural Award in 1999. Klein Dytham's stage design for rock band L'Arc en Ciel was another cooperative project. And in the case of the Tokyo Brewing Company, Namaiki handles the graphic design and Klein Dytham is responsible for the building that houses the brewery's bar. Countless projects revolve around the firms that make up Deluxe.

The 284-square-metre space has also hosted a spate of parties, exhibitions and other fascinating events. Nearly every other week a new music performance, installation or fashion show is the focus of attention at Deluxe. The English design group Tomato recently held a workshop on the premises, adding yet another dimension to the space. Particularly memorable was a 'wallpaper party' that the gang at Deluxe organised in October 1999. It was the culmination of several design-related events held in Tokyo that month, and judging by the crowd of people that showed up, virtually every designer, media personality and shop owner living in or visiting Tokyo was in attendance.

Although an ability to absorb, share and cross-fertilise is not limited to Klein Dytham, their skill in gathering together an impressively varied assortment of talented people is nothing if not indicative of KDa's overwhelming presence.
The hope of many of us fortunate enough to have savoured the Klein Dytham experience first-hand is that their exuberance will spark other designers to help them shape and maintain a full-fledged Tokyo design scene.

Chiharu Watabe is a Japanese design critic who lives in Tokyo.

prize

東京

i-mode >> internet >> www.i-fly.virgin.co.j

how to play

ヴァージン アトランティック航空

i-modeでクイズに答えて、ロンドンへ行

12月1日 → 12/ :00am →

quiz

design and co-ordination
+ www.klei
+ www.nam
+ www.gomag

site co-operation
+ veloqx city inve

Wonderwall (1)

After the enormous volume of free publicity generated by the Pika-Pika Pretzel project, Virgin Atlantic Airways asked KDa to mastermind another innovative ad campaign. Using the same hoarding location along Harajuku's fashionable Omotesando street, KDa developed an interactive billboard in conjunction with graphic design office Namaiki and Internet experts Goma Goma.

Restricted to a maximum of 35 per cent advertising coverage on the wall, KDa turned the whole wall into one big advert by making it in red acrylic, the distinctive Virgin colour. A 20-metre-long LED ticker-tape display was set into the wall. In operation throughout December 2000, the hoarding flashed a different general knowledge question each hour of the day. Passers-by with I-mode phones could enter the quiz by logging onto the campaign website. All correct entries went into a draw for that hour's prize or one of the monthly pool prizes, including one hundred return-flights to London. After each hour, entrants' mobile-phones automatically received an e-mail notifying them if they had answered the question correctly and whether or not they had won a prize.

Drawing on the Japanese love of technology in an imaginative and entertaining way, the project pioneered a new concept in advertising. It was the first time mobile phone technology had been used interactively for an outdoor advertisement. Judging by the curious onlookers at the time, the project certainly didn't go unnoticed.

Location: Jingumae, Shibuya-ku, Tokyo / Client: Virgin Atlantic Airways / Concept Design: Klein Dytham architecture, Namaiki / Graphic Design: Namaiki / I-mode Programming: Goma Goma / General Contractor: Inoue Industries / Start Design: July 2000 / Completion: December 2000 / Length: 20 metres / Wall: red acrylic sheets, LED ticker-tape / Photography: Katsuhisa Kida

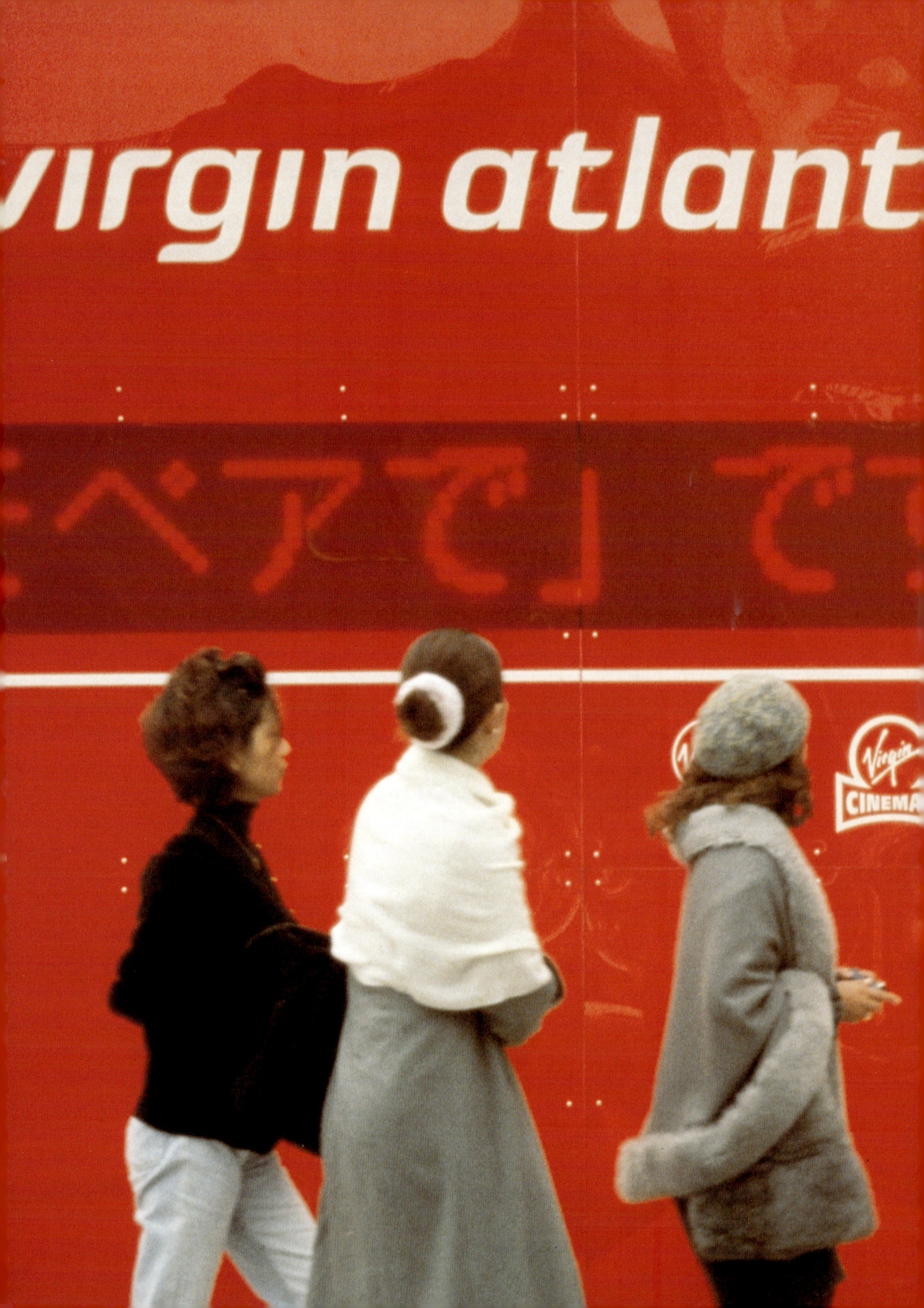
virgin atlant
ベアで」で
Virgin
CINEMA

virgin atlantic

how to play

ヴァージン アトランティック航空
i-modeでクイズに答えて、ロンド...
12月1日 → 12月...日 / 8:00am...pm

Bibliography

2001
- 'Casual! Architecture: 30 x 10 Architects' in Studio Voice, May, 43
- Barrie, Andrew, 'I-FLY Virgin' in Monument, April-May, 40-41
- 'Mi Piace il Design Italiano' in be Sure, April, 11
- 'Come on - a Sony house' in Brutus, 15 March, 25-28
- Iketani, Shuichi, 'My private museum' in Esquire, March, 50-51
- Barrie, Andrew, 'Universal Building Blocks' in Monument, February-March, 28
- Watabe, Chiharu, '100 key people of culture in the 21st century' in SPA!, 10 January, 7
- 'Bleacher Seat' in Wired, January

2000
- Din, Rasshied, ed. New Retail. Conran Octopus Limited, 174-177
- 'Cross view interview – I-FLY Virgin campaign' in Original Confidence, 18 December, 24
- 'My favorite product' in Pen, 1 December, 56
- 'Organic Design - amazing products' in Studio Voice, November, 29, 45
- 'Svenska formgivare sitter fint i Japan' in Svenska Dagbladet, 18 November, 18-19
- 'Tokyo Quake - deep into Tokyo's 14 creative mines' in Composite, November, 46-47, 65
- '4 eyes better than 2 eyes' in Brutus, 1 November, separate volume, 24-25
- 'Process' in JA; The Japan Architect, Autumn, 94-103
- 'Re-cabling!' in 10+1, September No.21, 86-89
- 'My way, my style' in Crea, September, 124-125
- 'Design Driven' in Australian Style, August, 120-121
- 'Contemporary Craftsmen' in Free & Easy, August, 99-103
- 'Good choice good sense goods' in I'm home, Summer, 28-31
- Azuma, Michiyo, 'Garage cutting edge' in I'm home, Summer, 68-69
- 'Klein Dytham architecture Odaiba Navi ' in Casa Brutus, Summer, 24-25
- Knebel, Nikolaus, 'Having a good time' in ish, August, 93-98
- Thiemann, Robert, 'The Decline of Office at Home' in Frame, July-August, 59-63
- 'Form Follows Function' in Shukan Bunshun, July, 20
- Barrie, Andrew, 'Advertising Space' in Monument, June-July, 22-23
- 'Klein Dytham architecture Special Issue' in SD, June, 5-68
- 'Big in Japan' in Blueprint, June, 52-54
- Slessor, Catharine, 'Delight' in The Architectural Review, June, 98
- 'Wind up garage' in Shitsunai, May, 78-79
- 'Vrooom!' in Shinkenchiku, March, 168-171
- 'Vrooom!' in GA Japan, March-April, 84-88
- 'Gaizin Collectors' in Men's Ex, April, 162
- 'Trans-architecture' in A, February volume 6, 54-57

1999
- GAP ed. Creators File for LIVING. GAP Publication Co. Ltd, 78-81
- 'Y2Kb' in Monument, Millennium special issue, 40-41
- 'Project news-site' in Nikkei Architecture, December, 13, 30
- 'Deluxe Wallpaper Party' in Elle Deco, December, 126
- 'Deluxe - Sharing the space beyond specialties' in Design News, Winter, 68-69
- 'Men's hideout' in Esquire, December, 102-103, 107
- 'BBH' 'SinDen' in Shotekenchiku, November, 214-216, 217
- 'My Tokyo' in Hot Air (Virgin Atlantic in Flight Magazine), October-December, 98

i-mode >> intern... ...i-fly.virgin.co.jp

virgin

quiz

デジタルスクリーンで1時間... ...を出題。
答えがわかったら、i-mo...
1人1時間1回のチャンス。... ...i-modeにEメールでご連絡します。

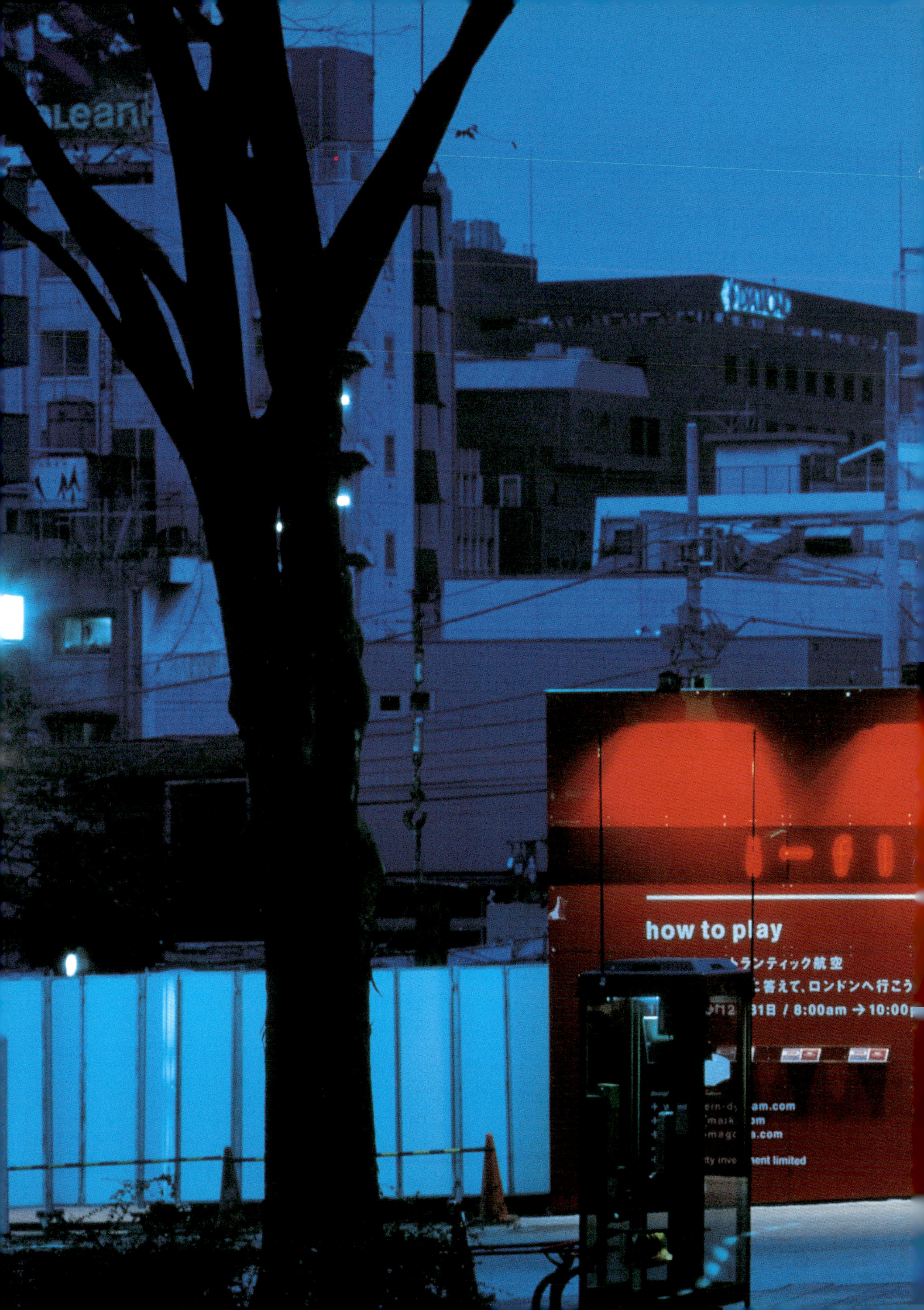
how to play
ランティック航空
に答えて、ロンドンへ行こう
31日 / 8:00am → 10:00

Wonderwall (2)

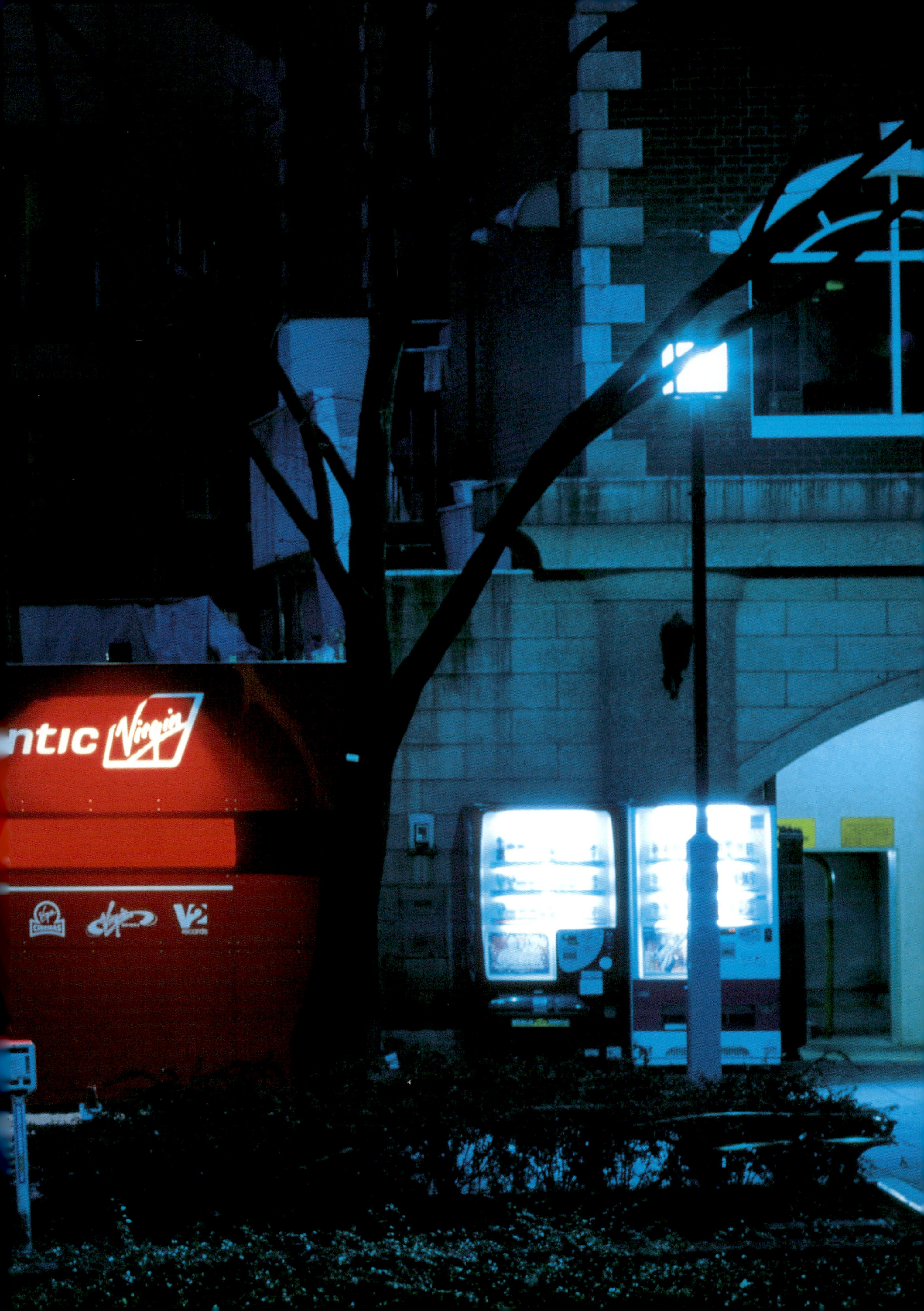
ntic Virgin

virgin at

prize
1ヶ月間で100名様に東京ーロンドン往復航空券
ヴァージン メガストア　商品券
ヴァージン シネマズ1年パス
ヴァージン・コーラ1年分
アンダーワールド グッズ

- Elephant Design, 'Ku-so Kaden / form follows function+frills' in Design News, Autumn, 66-67
- 'Tokyo renovation' in SD, October, 26-29
- 'Office interior' in Elle Deco, October, 118-119
- 'Be careful of Brits!' in Soto Koto, October, 24-27
- 'Brewing up in Tokyo' in Blueprint, September, 18
- Watabe, Chiharu, 'Deeper into the digital age' in Frame, August-September, 58-63
- 'Designer 6-Pack' in Monument, June-July, 20
- 'Deluxe' in Asahi evening news, June, 11, 24
- 'Deluxe humor...' in SD, May, 136-137
- 'Ideal hiding place' in Men's Ex, April, 129
- 'Deluxe' in Koukoku, January-February, 48, 71
- 'Couples in Vogue' in Vogue Nippon
- 'A factory in Tokyo - Deluxe' in Ryuko-Tsushin

1998

- 'Flush: Kamban shelter' in Nikkei Architecture, 23 November, 141-143
- 'The British Council information centre' in Shotenkenchiku, August, 194-195
- 'Close Up: British Council' in Shitsunai, August, 84-85
- 'Angle: Klein Dytham's void furniture' in Shotenkenchiku, May, 202-204
- 'New Design Environments Through Unit Activities' in SD, April, 39-44
- 'Smile Baloon - UK98 pavilion' in GA Japan, March-April No.31, 170-173
- 'Code' in Shotenkenchiku, March, 111-114
- Jeffs, Angela, 'King of Solutions, Color Queen' in The Japan Times, 22 February
- 'Furniture detail' in Shitsunai, February, 86-89, interview on 56-59

1997

- 'La Ciocca' in Shotenkenchiku, December, 153-155
- Fujisaki & Hirabayashi, 'Soho living space study' in Brutus, 15 November, 90-91
- 'Hong Kong 1997 The Accelerating City' in SD, July, 18-19
- 'Furniture detail' in Shitsunai, June, 79-82
- 'Work from Tokyo' in Idea, May, 86-89
- 'Visiting a studio' in Shitsunai, April, 87-97
- 'Beyond borders' in Nikkei Architecture, January, 13, 87

1996

- 'Idée's new corner shop' in Blueprint, December, 24-25
- 'What's new - new material MOW' in Shinkenchiku, November, 122-123
- 'Idée Workstation' in Shotenkenchiku, September, 99-102
- 'News architecture - Idée Workstation' in Nikkei Architecture, 9 September, 27-32

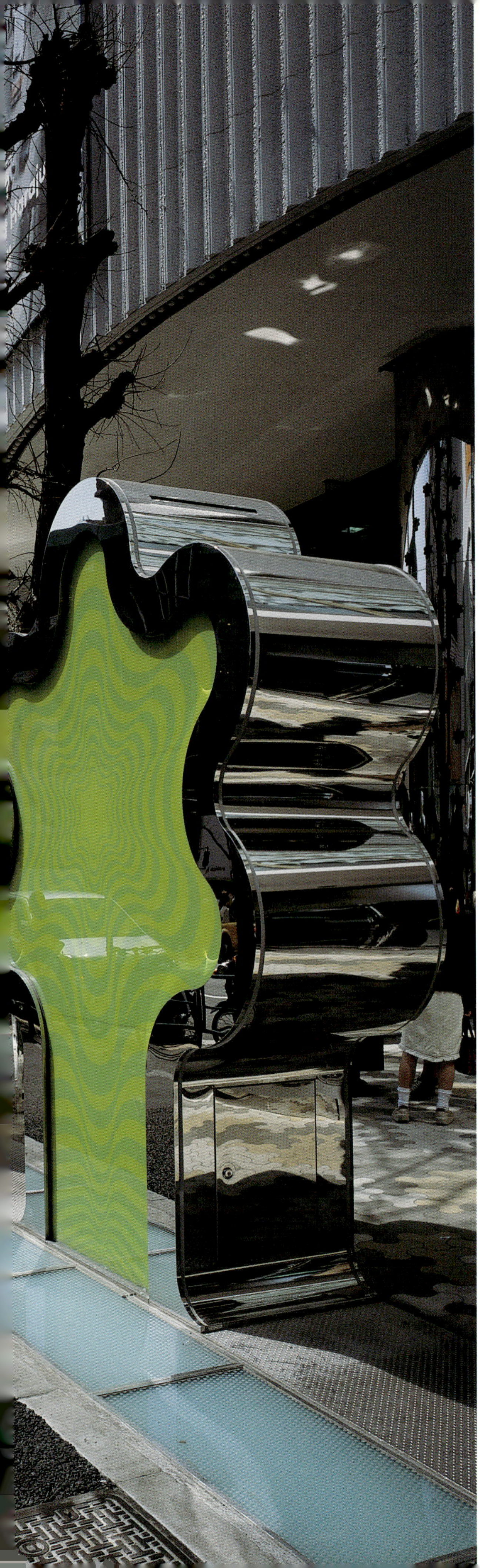

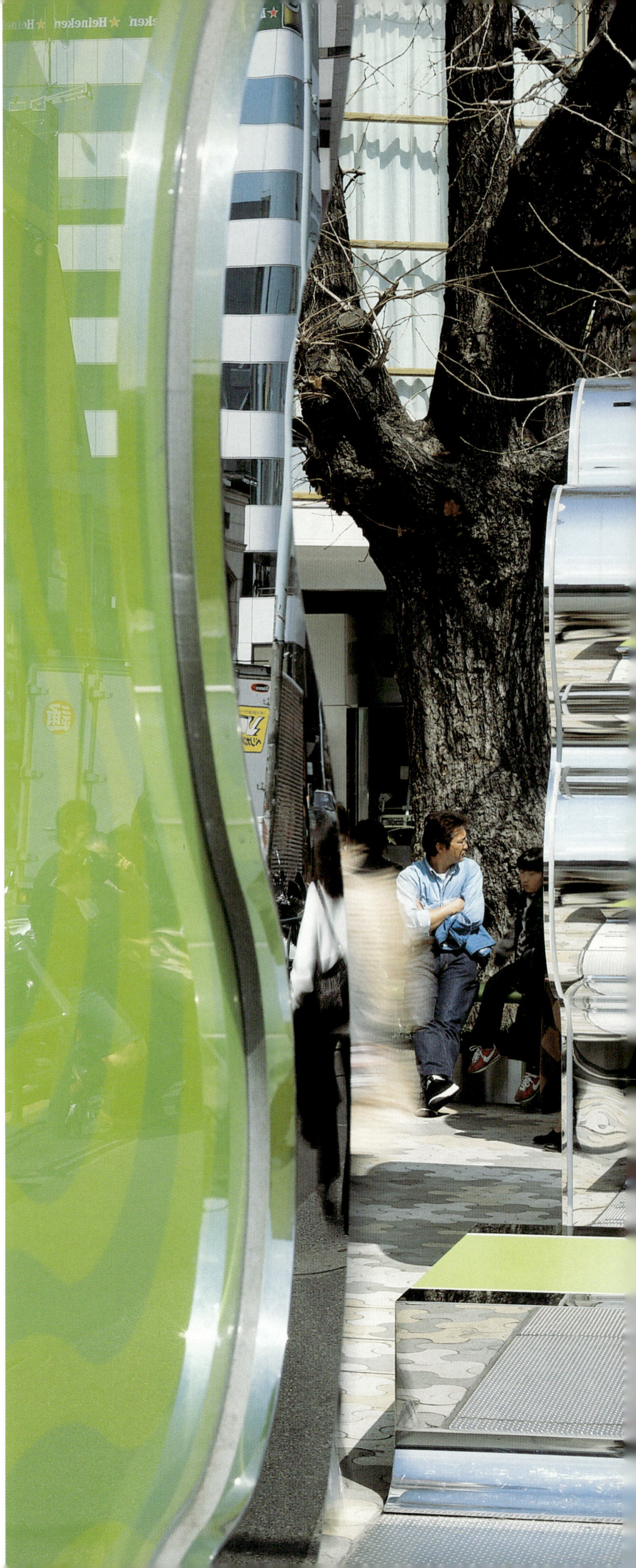

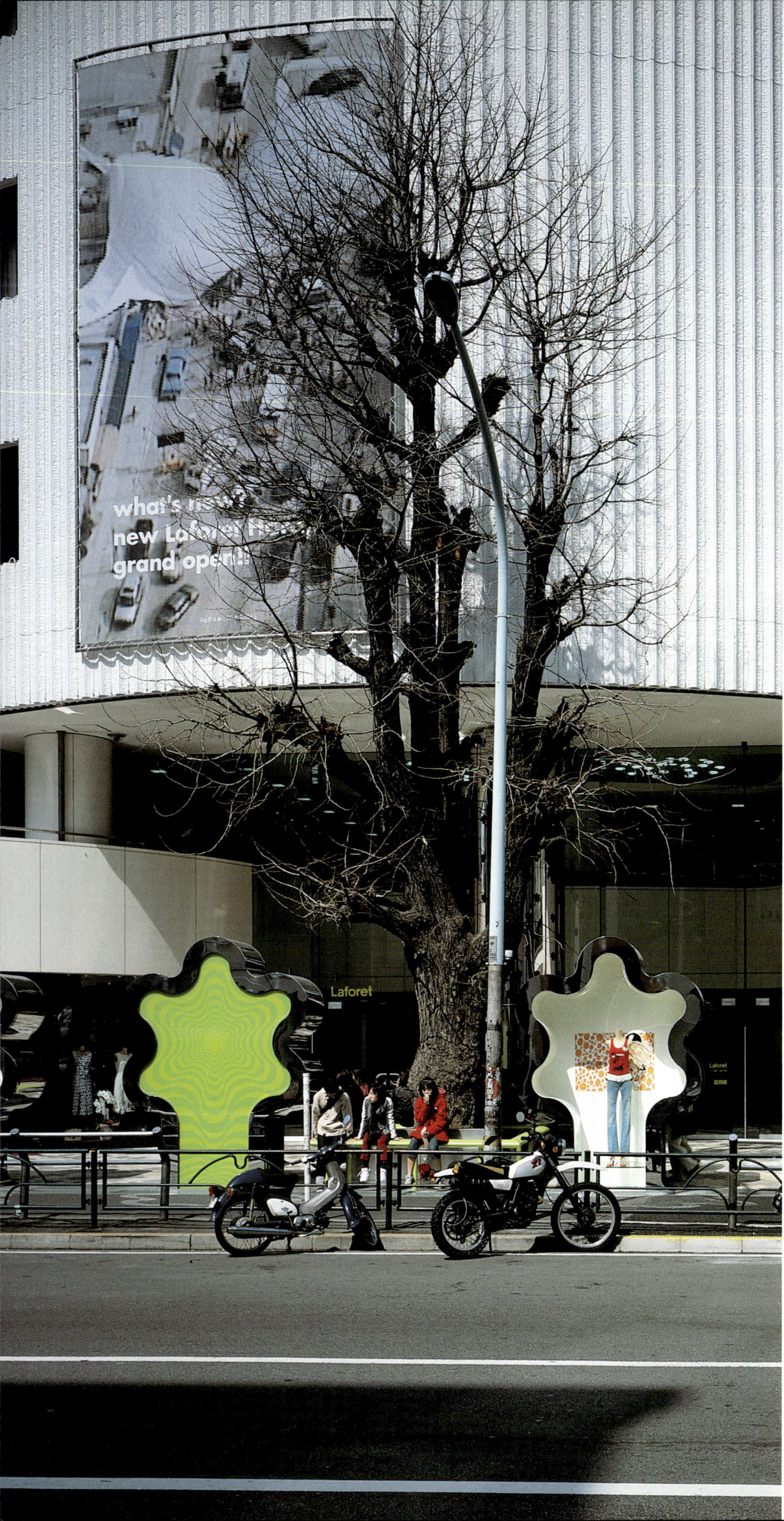
Laforet

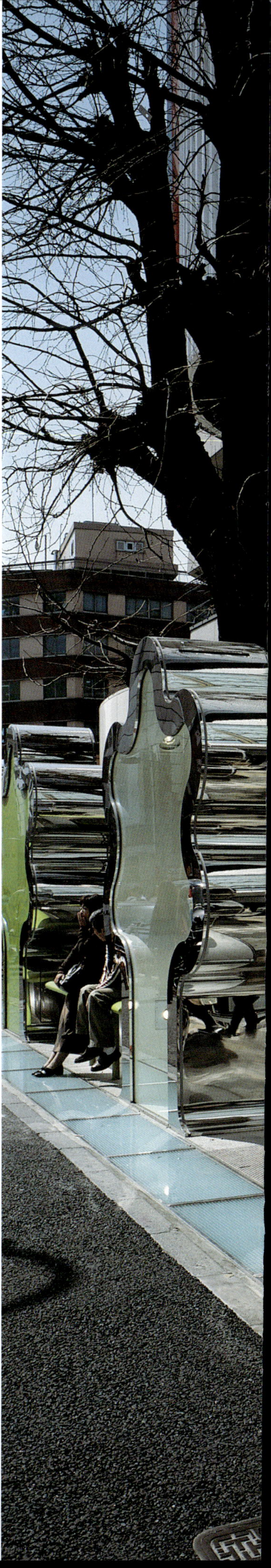

Rin-Rin (1)

It's not difficult to see what KDa had in mind when redesigning this Mecca for Tokyo's fashionable youth: trees, forest, and plenty of green. Not in any natural or scenic way, though. The materials used are plastic, polished stainless steel, and tiles.

Along the 50-metre street frontage they 'planted' a row of tree-shaped objects. The stainless steel sweeps up from the ground like a ribbon, forms a tree, skirts along the ground and then forms the next tree. Made of polished stainless-steel mirrors, the trees come in handy for the image-conscious crowd gathering in front of this trendy fashion palace. They also act as light-boxes for graphics and as showcases for fashion displays.

The line of trees is emphasised by a glass strip set in the ground, illuminated from below. Light fibres installed at the front of the building can change colour to suit any occasion. Given the rocketing costs, the effectiveness of this 'world-wide-first' lighting system is impressive indeed.

The tree motif was inspired by Laforet, the French name of the department store, derived originally from the owner's name Mori, Japanese for forest. The word consists of three tree characters. With this in mind, KDa added another tree character and came up with the new word rin-rin, meaning 'little woods'. KDa was also prompted by the plane trees in front of Laforet, removed to make way for construction of a new subway line.

A big stainless-steel column in front of the entrance is – in a tribute to designer Alessi – perforated by tree shapes. The entrance area is faced with specially designed three-pronged ceramic tiles – called 'rin-rin' tiles – with a distinct camouflage colour pattern.

Inside, KDa gave the space of the department store a much lighter, airy and uncluttered feeling. Whitish materials, curved retro-lining for all surfaces, with accents in polished mirror and a bright seedling green, give the interior a youthful and fresh look, just like the fashion articles on sale at Laforet.

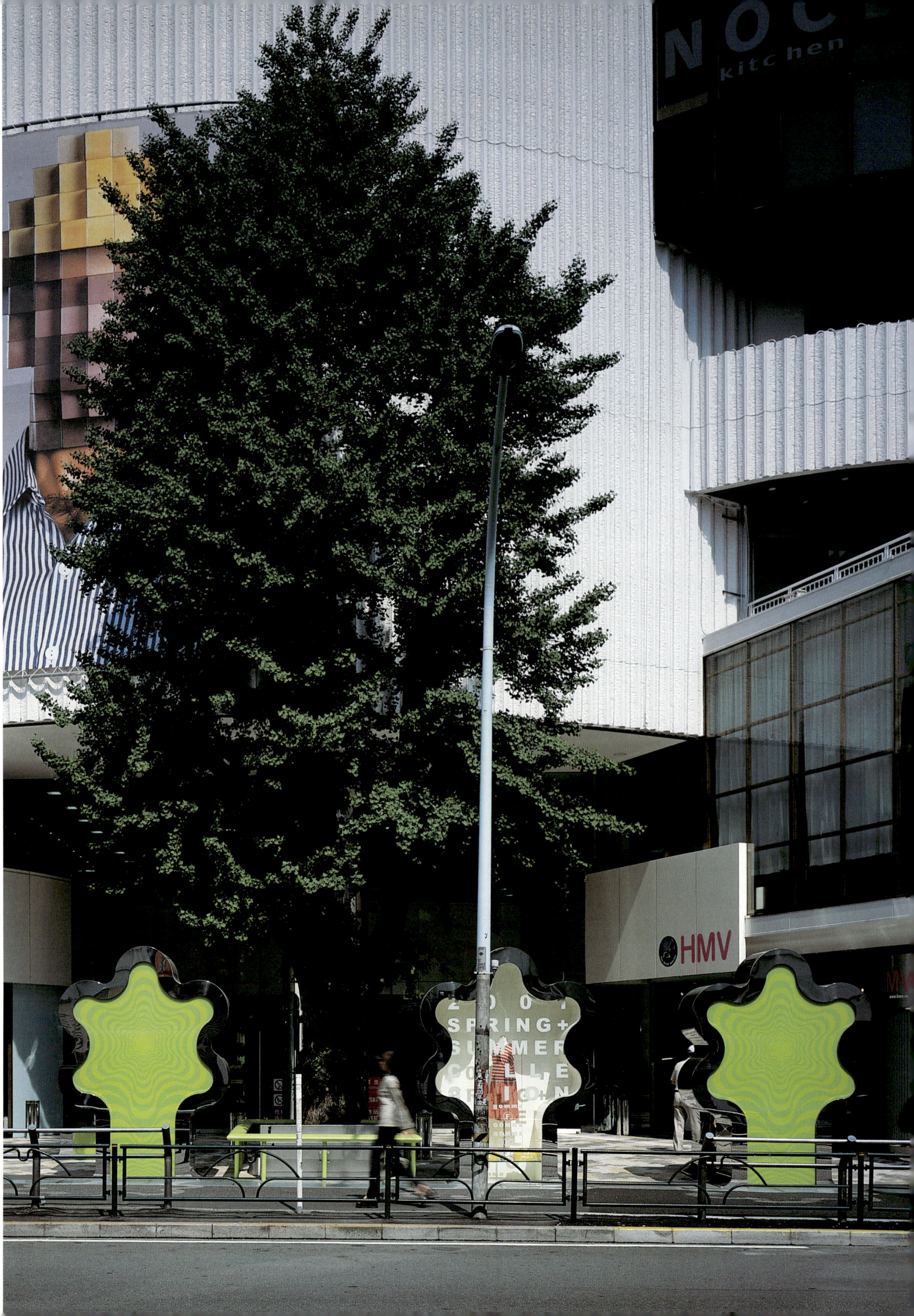
kitchen
HMV
SPRING+
SUMMER

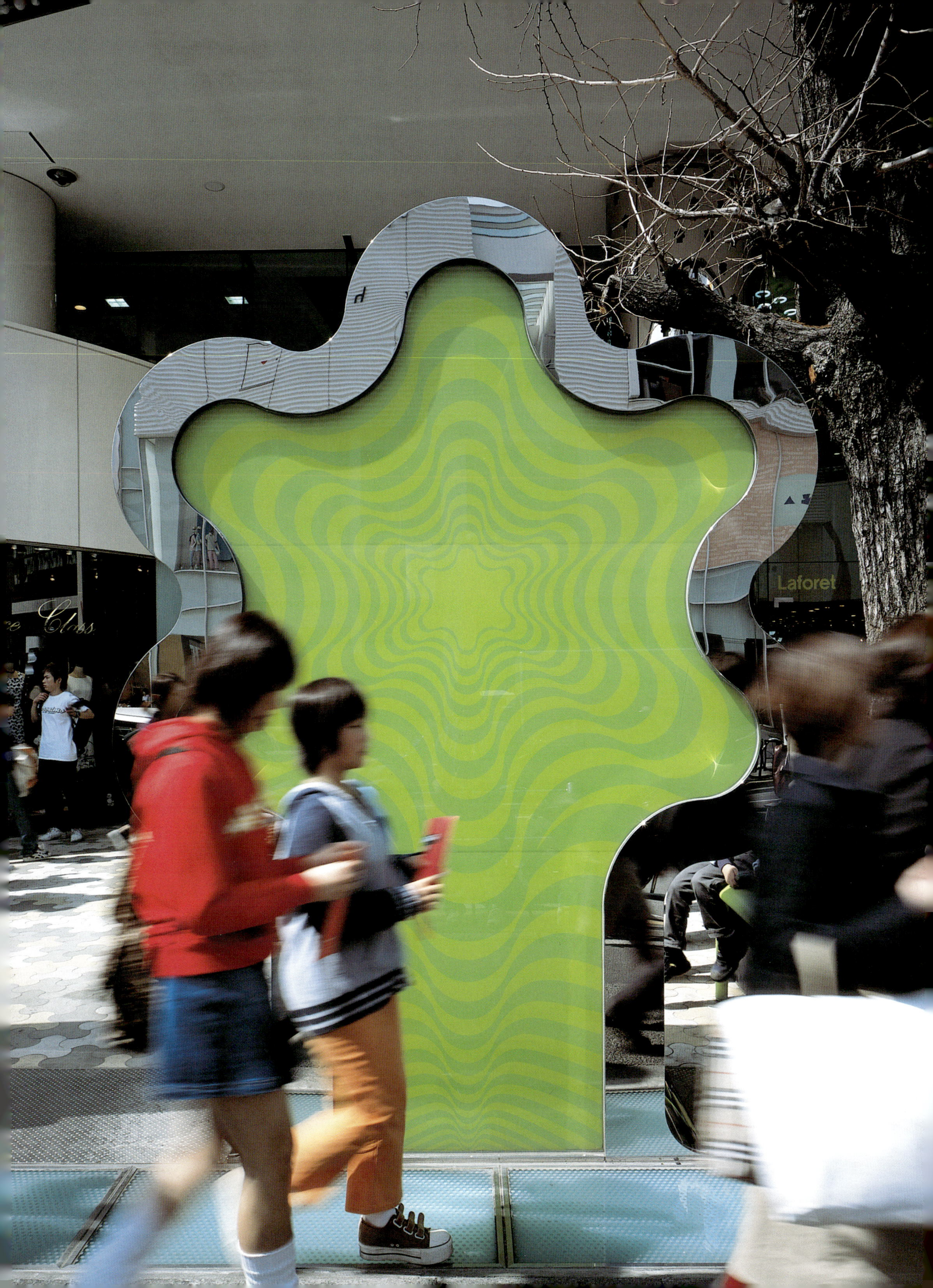
Laforet

Colophon

Klein Dytham architecture – Tokyo Calling
Frame Monographs of Contemporary Interior Architects

Publishers • Frame Publishers – www.framemag.com
Birkhäuser – Publishers for Architecture – www.birkhauser.ch
Concept • De Designpolitie – www.designpolitie.nl
Compilation • Carolien van Tilburg, with contributions by Deyan Sudjic, Toyo Ito and Chiharu Watabe
Graphic Design • www.designpolitie.nl
Copy editing • Donna de Vries-Hermansader, Billy Nolan
Translation • InOtherWords: Donna de Vries-Hermansader, Billy Nolan
Production • Tessa Blokland/Frame magazine
Colour reproduction • Graphic Link
Printing • Hoonte Bosch & Keuning

Sponsored by • D. Brain Co. Ltd

Distribution • Benelux, China, Japan, Korea and Taiwan
ISBN 90-806445-1-X
BIS Publishers
P.O. Box 15751
NL-1001 NG Amsterdam
The Netherlands
www.bispublishers.nl

All other countries
ISBN 3-7643-6559-5
Birkhäuser – Publishers for Architecture
P.O. Box 133
CH-4010 Basel
Switzerland
Member of the BertelsmannSpringer Publishing Group
www.birkhauser.ch

Copyright © 2001 Frame
Copyright © 2001 Birkhäuser

A CIP catalogue record for this book is available from the Library of Congress, Washington D.C., USA

Deutsche Bibliothek Cataloging-in-Publication Data
Klein Dytham Architecture <Tōkyō>:
Klein Dytham Architecture / Frame Magazine, Amsterdam.
[Transl. in other words: Donna de Vries-Hermansader]. -
Basel ; Boston ; Berlin : Birkhäuser, 2001
(Frame monographs of contemporary interior architects)
ISBN 3-7643-6559-5

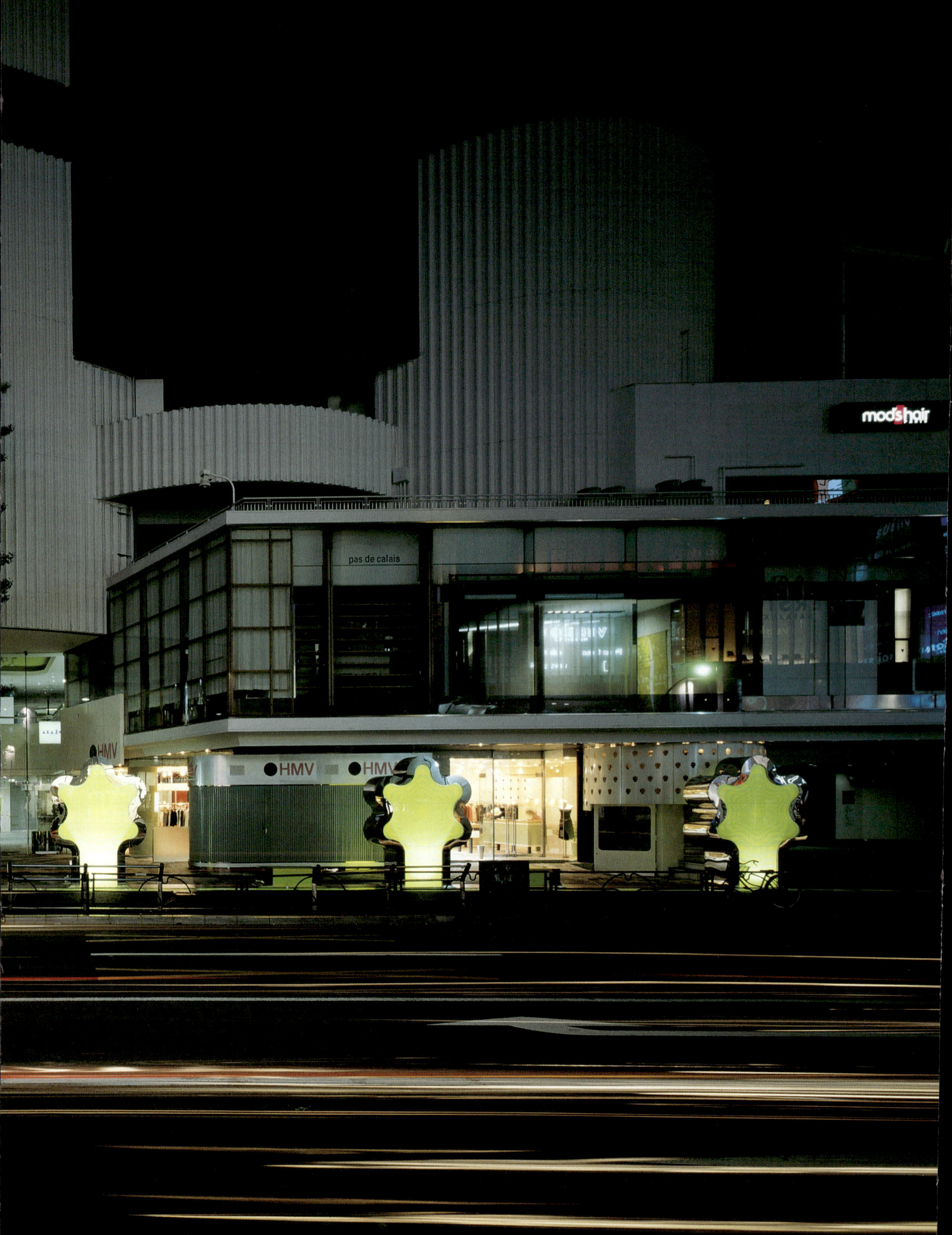

mod's hair
pas de calais
HMV
HMV
HMV

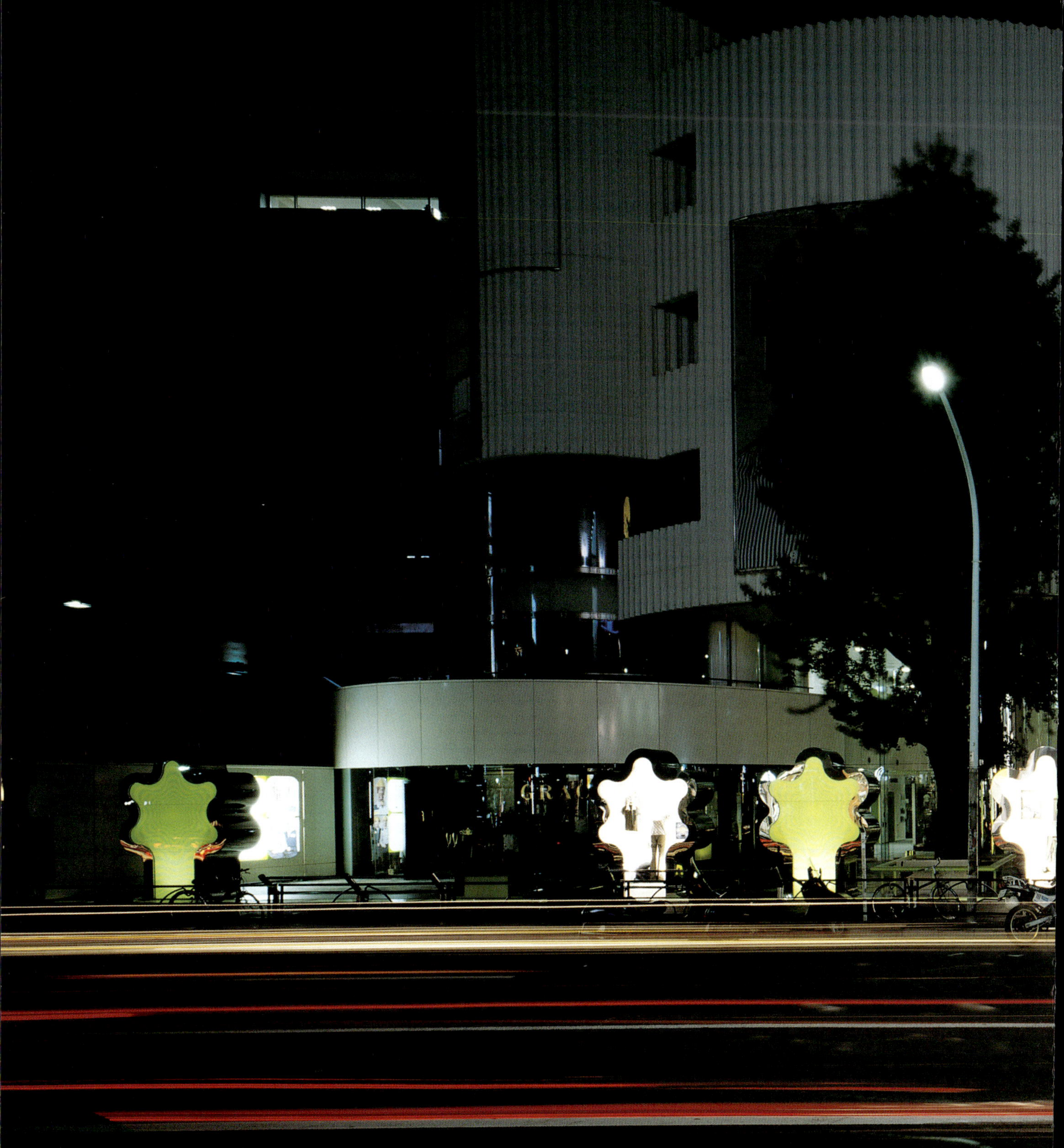

Rin-Rin (2)

Location: Laforet Harajuku, Jingumae, Shibuya-ku, Tokyo / Client: Mori Building Ryutsu System Co. Ltd / General Contractor: Ishizue Co. Ltd / Start Design: October 2000 / Open: March 2001 / Floor Area: 819 square metres / Floor: ceramic tile designed by KDa, illuminated glass floor / Trees: mirrored stainless steel, laminated glass / Photography: Katsuhisa Kida

LAFORET MUSEUM
NOCE
LUCKY STRIKE
NAUTICA
BRUTUS
ソニーが車を作ったよ!?
THE KING CLINIC
Love Beer?
P

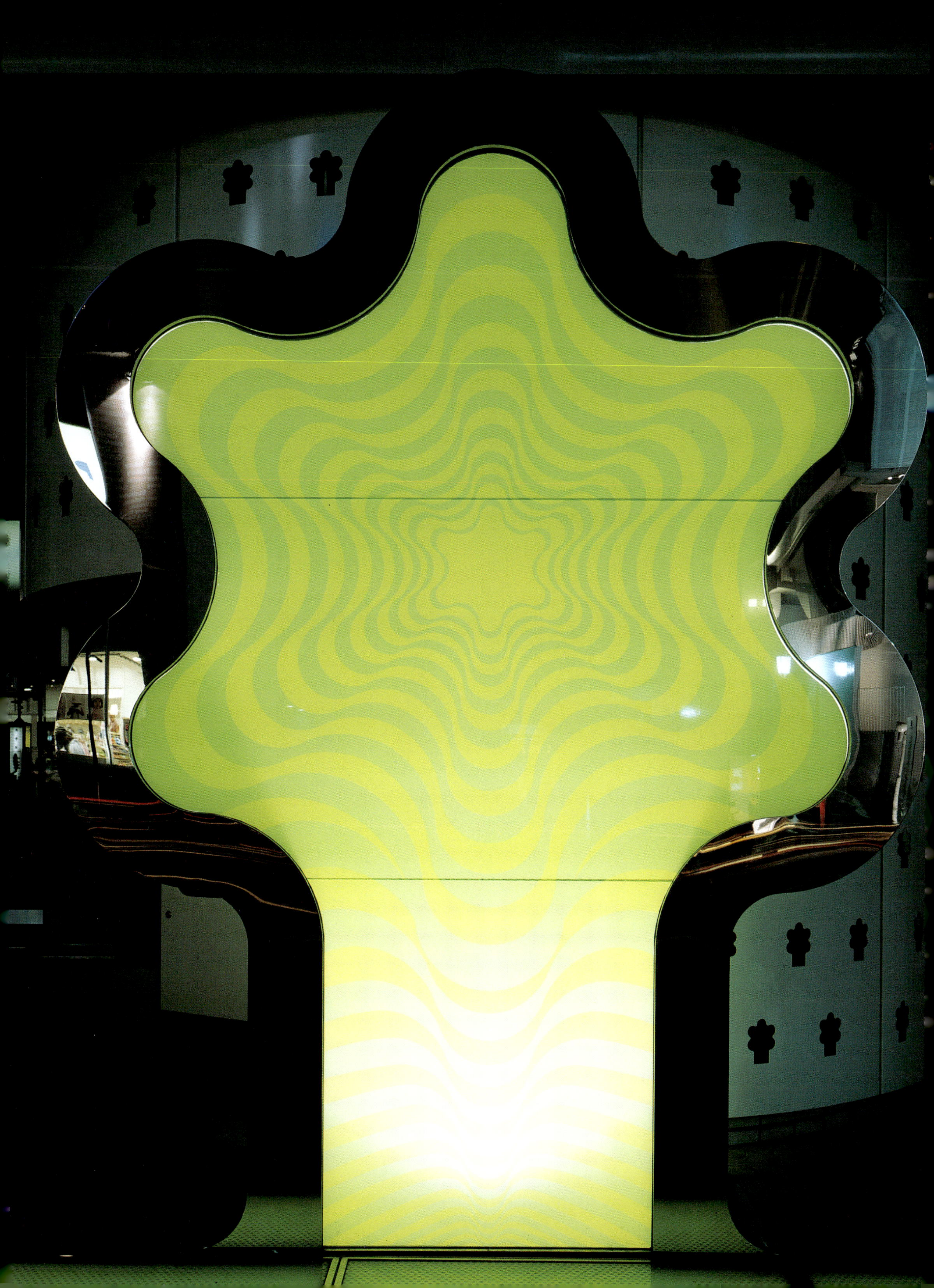

Copyrights on the photographs, illustrations, drawings and written material in this publication are owned by the respective photographers, the graphic designer, the (interior) architects and their clients, and the authors.

This work is subject to copyright. All rights are reserved, whether the whole or part of the material is concerned, specifically the rights of translation, reprinting, re-use of illustrations, recitation, broadcasting, reproduction on microfilms or in other ways, and storage in data bases. For any kind of use, permission of the copyright owner must be obtained.

Printed in the Netherlands
987654321

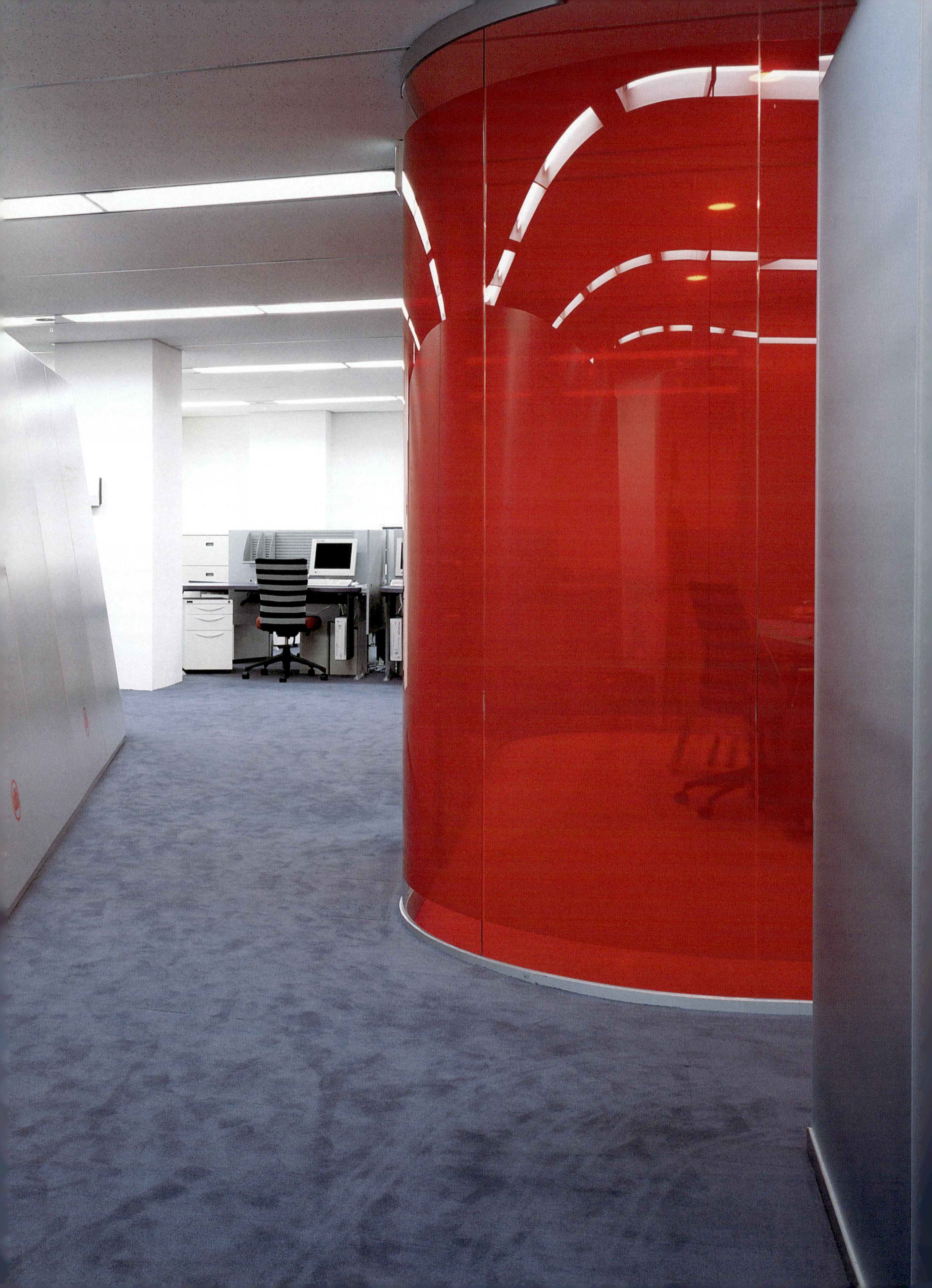

IN CASE OF URGENT PHOTOCOPY
CUT HERE

Virgin Atlantic Airways Office

The customer area at Virgin Atlantic Airways looks like a small, red gift box placed under a conventional office building. The glazed box, with curved corners and covered with red film, reveals only a glimpse of what is going on in the back office. The red reflects Virgin's brand image, while the purple counter forms a vivid contrast with the rest of the tiny space.

A slightly slanting aluminium wall, also with rounded edges, closes off part of the office from the storage and customer box. In form, this functional installation echoes the shell of an aeroplane. Although at first sight the open-plan workspace looks like an average office, the ergonomically curved tabletops and upholstery of the office chairs bear the unmistakable hand of KDa.

Location: Minami Aoyama, Minato-ku, Tokyo / Client: Virgin Atlantic Airways Ltd / General Contractor: D. Brain Co. Ltd / Start Design: January 2001 / Open: May 2001 / Furniture: OXO seating (Hitch Mylius) for entrance, T-chair (Vitra) for working area, custom-built working desks (Schiavello Japan) / Wall: coloured film on glass for reception area, wing-shape silver-coated steel partition / Photography: Katsuhisa Kida